GREAT AMERICAN QUILTS 1988

GREAT AMERICAN QUILTS 1988

Compiled and Edited by

Sandra L. O'Brien

© 1988 by Oxmoor House, Inc.
Book Division of Southern Progress Corporation
P.O. Box 2463, Birmingham, Alabama 35201

Library of Congress Catalog Number: 86-62283
ISBN: 0-8487-0720-6
ISSN: 0890-8222
Manufactured in the United States of America
First Printing 1988

Executive Editor: Candace N. Conard
Production Manager: Jerry Higdon
Associate Production Manager: Rick Litton
Art Director: Bob Nance

Great American Quilts 1988

Editor: Sandra L. O'Brien
Editorial Assistant: Margaret Allen Northen
Production Assistant: Theresa L. Beste
Copy Chief: Mary Jean Haddin
Designer: Yukie Kodaira McLean
Cover Designer: Earl Freedle
Artist: Larry Hunter
Photographers: Gary Clark, Beth Maynor, Colleen Duffley, Mary-Gray Hunter, Howard L. Puckett, Jim Bathie, Courtland Richards
Poems: Sandra L. O'Brien

Special thanks to Frank Stella for permission to use his name on Ruth Yarbrough's quilt, *Frank Stella I,* found on page 10.

CONTENTS

EDITOR'S NOTE

I've never met a quilter who didn't have a heap of fabric scraps somewhere. Whether they're stashed away in the darkest crevices of the hall closet or neatly stacked in plastic containers, these fabric leftovers are ready when called—to be whipped into the finest of quilts. Throw them away? Never!—despite bulging boxes and meager storage space. In our special chapter, "Scraps to Spare," you will meet several quilters who wedded their scraps to make some fabulous quilts.

Skillful quilters with generous hearts populate our "Quilts Across America" chapter. They welcome you into their quilting lives by telling you a little about themselves. Their joy in quilting spills over into the lovely quilts they make.

Blissful childhood memories of relatives and neighbors quilting are recalled by quilters in our "Traditions in Quilting" chapter. Accounts of how quilting has intertwined their family tree are shared, along with their quilts.

Our "Bee Quilters" chapter found quilting guilds as busy as ever. While you make one of their quilts, read about their quiltmaking methods for groups of quilters and about their many quilt-related philanthropic projects.

Footlighted in our "Designer Gallery" are the quilting imaginations of some multi-talented quilters. Browse through the gallery and be inspired by their ability to manipulate fabrics and colors in ingenious ways. Quilters are always striving to make their quilting the best it can be. And many are experimenting and incorporating techniques from all facets of the art world into their quilting. Fabric hand dyeing and screen printing are two examples. To accommodate your needs, we have included a list of resources for books, pamphlets, supplies, and fabrics in these areas to aid quilters in locating these sometimes hard-to-find materials.

Most important, take a few minutes to read our Preliminary Instructions. This year we are featuring a brief review of some frequently used appliquéing techniques. It may be a refresher course for some, but we hope it will be of help to you, no matter how long you have been a quilter.

Quilting means so much to quilters. It is the one activity that they repeatedly tell me releases the tension, provides the creative outlet and the extra money, satisfies the need for achievement, and makes the day go well. The list goes on and on. I am always touched by these ovations to quilting.

One in particular is the story of Mrs. Gladys Burkett of Monroeville, Alabama. Mrs. Burkett suffered a stroke at the age of 72 and underwent brain surgery. As her daughter told us, "She was left very weak and with very frequent and severe headaches." Shortly after leaving the hospital, Mrs. Burkett's sister introduced her to lap quilting. "Some days," explains her daughter, "she doesn't feel well enough to get up, but she manages somehow to quilt in bed, even on her bad days." She chooses patterns with small pieces and places a board on her lap to cut them. Using a small circular hoop for quilting, Mrs. Burkett has completed over 40 quilts in the five years since her illness. "She is grateful for this creative outlet," says her daughter, "and we are so proud of her determined spirit."

This is the spirit we so frequently find within each quilter. We are glad so many of you have shared it with us in *Great American Quilts*.

Preliminary Instructions

All pattern pieces include ¼″ seam allowance. All measurements for pieces and sashing and border strips are given with seam allowances. Some oversize pieces are placed on a grid, with scale information noted. (See Enlarging a Pattern from a Grid below.)

Fabric requirements are based on 44″-45″-wide fabric with trimmed selvages. Please note that generous fabric allowances are given for fabric requirements to account for fabric shrinkage and individual differences in fabric cutting. Fabric requirements are given for one-piece borders and continuous bias strips. Finished quilt size is the size of the quilt before quilting.

Prepare fabrics before marking and cutting by washing, drying, and pressing.

Enlarging a Pattern From a Grid

Grid Size: 1 square equals 1″.
1. Prepare a grid of 1″ squares.
2. Number squares vertically and horizontally on both the pattern and your grid. Use the numbers as a guide to copy the pattern outline from the original, square by square. Now the pattern is ready for template making.

Appliquéing

Quite a few methods exist for appliquéing. Here is a summary of those most frequently used by quilters. Choose one that you feel comfortable with and one that produces the best results for you. (Quiltmaking instructions for each quilt that follows contain the method preferred by that particular quilter.)

Machine-Stitched Appliqué — There are several methods:
1. Fuse appliqué piece to background fabric with lightweight fusible or paper-backed adhesive web. This stabilizes the piece on the background and makes machine stitching easier, especially if the piece has a lot of curves. Cover raw edges with a satin stitch.
2. Or anchor the piece to the background fabric by machine-basting on the seam line. Carefully trim excess fabric outside seam line. Cover machine basting with a satin stitch.
3. Using lightweight fusible interfacing is also popular with some. Apply a piece of lightweight fusible interfacing to appliqué piece. Anchor piece to background using a glue stick. Cover raw edges with a satin stitch.

Hand-Stitched Appliqué — In general, guidelines to remember for hand-stitched appliquéing are as follows: If the appliquéd edge can be pried up with your fingernail, the stitches are too far apart. And the finished size of your background fabric should be the same size as it was before appliquéing.

These tips may make your hand-stitched appliquéing easier:
1. Before appliquéing, clip inside curves and angles as close to the seam line as possible. The steeper the curve, the closer the clippings should be to each other. Stitch inside (concave) curves first. Trim seam allowances of points to prevent fabric from bunching underneath.
2. Some quilters machine-stitch on the seam line of each piece before appliquéing. This makes turning the seam allowance under easier, gives a cleaner edge, and makes the piece lie flat.
3. An invisible appliqué stitch is recommended by many quilters. See Ami Simms's *Whig Rose* for stitching directions.

SCRAPS TO SPARE

Like cherished friendships, my favorite snatches,
*   a host of fragments in a woven basket.*
My frugal instincts continually at work,
*   yearn to give all things some value and some worth.*
Small detached pieces, waiting to be bound,
*   —never lost but glad to be found.*
I'm glad I never threw them away;
*   my scraps of yore are my quilts today.*

Ruth Yarbrough

Imperial Beach, California

Three years ago, Ruth attended a quilting group at a local library and has been producing excellent quilts ever since. "I find quilting to be a very satisfying medium," says Ruth. "I have tried painting, ceramics, enameling, and other art forms, but I enjoy quilting the most."

Fascinated and inspired by the paintings of the contemporary painter Frank Stella, Ruth has been absorbed in her own quilted renditions of his paintings. She recently completed a second quilt, *Frank Stella II,* and we look forward to seeing more series quilts from Ruth.

Frank Stella Quilt I
1985
Inspired by Frank Stella's painting, *Sharpesville,* Ruth organized squares of scrap fabrics within larger concentric squares, in much the same way as Stella organizes many of his paintings. After piecing more than 3,000 scrap squares, Ruth transformed them into three-dimensional waves of color by diagonal cross-hatched quilting. "I get a wonderful feeling when I see a pieced top change to the lovely contours of quilting," says Ruth.

Many quilters will enjoy individually piecing squares, a process which allows them the freedom to select exact color locations as Ruth did. But dedicated strip-piecers can easily adjust the instructions by making several strip sections of six 1½"-wide strips. Be sure to make sections with different scraps to vary color combinations. Cut across each strip at 1½" increments and join in rows as indicated in Steps 1, 2, 4, 6, and 8.

Frank Stella Quilt I

Finished Quilt Size
74" x 74"

Fabric Requirements

Scrap fabrics	—5¼ yd. total
Muslin	—2¼ yd.
Bias binding	—1¼ yd.
Backing	—4¼ yd.

Number to Cut

Square	—3,396 scrap fabrics

Quilt Top Assembly

1. Start with center section and piece 36 scrap squares to form one large pieced square. (See Quilt Assembly Diagram I.) Cut 4 strips, 1½" wide, from muslin. Join to sides of pieced square in log cabin fashion.

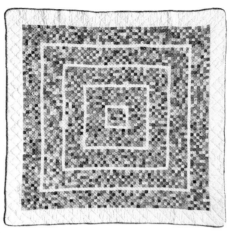

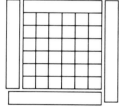

Quilt Assembly Diagram I

2. Piece 336 scrap squares in rows of 6 squares each. Join 20 rows for side section. (See Quilt Assembly Diagram II.) Make 2 side sections. Join 8 rows for top section and 8 rows for bottom section. Join top and bottom sections to center section and then side sections. (See Quilt Assembly Diagram II.)

Top Section

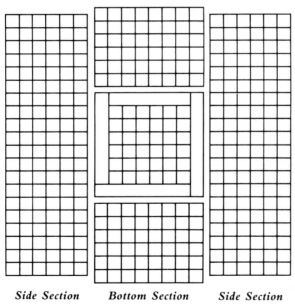

Side Section   *Bottom Section*   *Side Section*

Quilt Assembly Diagram II

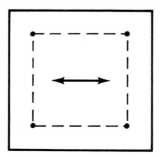

3. Cut 4 strips, 1½" wide, from muslin. Join to quilt in log cabin fashion.

4. Piece 672 scrap squares in rows of 6 squares each, as before. Join 34 rows for side section. Make 2 side sections. Join 22 rows for top section and 22 rows for bottom section. Join top and bottom sections to quilt and then side sections as done in Step 2.

5. Cut 4 strips, 1½" wide, from muslin. Join to quilt in log cabin fashion, as before.

6. Piece 1,008 scrap squares in rows of 6 squares each. Join 48 rows for side section. Make 2 side sections. Join 36 rows for top section and 36 rows for bottom section. Join top and bottom sections to quilt and then side sections.

7. Cut 4 strips, 1½" wide, from muslin. Join to quilt in log cabin fashion, as before.

8. Piece 1,344 scrap squares in rows of 6 squares each. Join 62 rows for side section. Make 2 side sections. Join 50 rows for top section and 50 rows for bottom section. Join top and bottom sections to quilt and then side sections.

9. Cut 2 strips, 6½" wide, from muslin and join to top and bottom of quilt. Cut 2 strips, 6½" wide, from muslin and join to quilt sides.

Quilting

Ruth quilted a ¾" cross-hatching pattern running across the diagonals of each square, with the exception of the 6" border strips. Border strips are quilted in 3" diamond squares. Outline-quilt along outside edge of last scrap-pieced section.

Finished Edges

Round corners and bind with a continuous bias strip of your favorite scrap fabric.

While growing up in Kyoto, Japan, Emiko acquired a fondness for handwork and a special attraction to traditional Japanese fabrics and designs. "Quiltmaking for me has been an ideal synthesis of these things and many more," says Emiko. "It is totally suited to my needs for self-expression." She considers her quilts to be original transformations of traditional patterns. This talented quilter especially enjoys the designing because, as she says, "I can express myself most freely." As a professional quilter, Emiko has frequently exhibited her quilts, her most recent show being a solo exhibition in New York City.

Emiko Toda Loeb
New York, New York

Bohkyoh
1984

This is the first of a series of quilts in which Emiko applies the idea of replicating weaving patterns on a large scale. "I have long been fascinated by the idea of imposing (or superimposing) irregular patterns onto the basic log cabin structure," says Emiko.

Bohkyoh is a reversible quilt that contains scraps from over 100 different traditional Japanese fabrics known as *aizome*. These are Japanese cotton fabrics dyed with indigo, either prior to weaving or by using a stencil on the fabric. *Aizome* can be purchased from specialty fabric stores. (See "Resources" for ordering information.) Of course, Emiko acknowledges, this quilt can be made using fabrics from your scrap bag—hers just happened to contain Japanese fabrics.

The Cornerstone Log Cabin block is used on the front and the Traditional Swirling Log Cabin block on the back. Many of you will want to duplicate Emiko's setting on the front, while others may prefer a less complicated setting with only one type of Cornerstone block on the front. Directions are given for both. Emiko recommends that all design and fabric choices be made before beginning work.

Bohkyoh (reversible)

Finished Quilt Size
55½" x 73½"

Number of Blocks and Finished Size
48 reversible blocks—9" x 9"

Fabric Requirements
Scraps for Cornerstone
blocks (includes yardage
for front binding)—6½ yd.
total★
Contrast scraps for
squares in
Cornerstone
blocks — 1 yd. total
Yellow (includes yardage
for back binding)—2¼ yd.
Contrast scraps
for Traditional
Spiraling blocks — 1¾ yd.
total★★

★ — A 12" x 14" rectangle of fabric
will provide strips for one Cornerstone block.
★★ — A 14" square of *scrap* fabric
will provide strips for four Traditional Spiraling blocks to make one
unit. (See Quilt Settings I and II.)

Quilt Assembly
1. Since this is a reversible quilt,
the front and back are made simultaneously. Refer to the Quilt Settings and decide on a setting and
placement of fabrics before beginning. Quilt Setting I requires several variations of the Cornerstone
block. Front and back blocks have
the same block numbers.

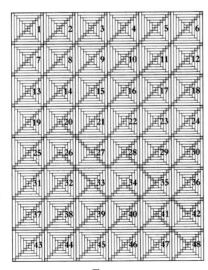

Front

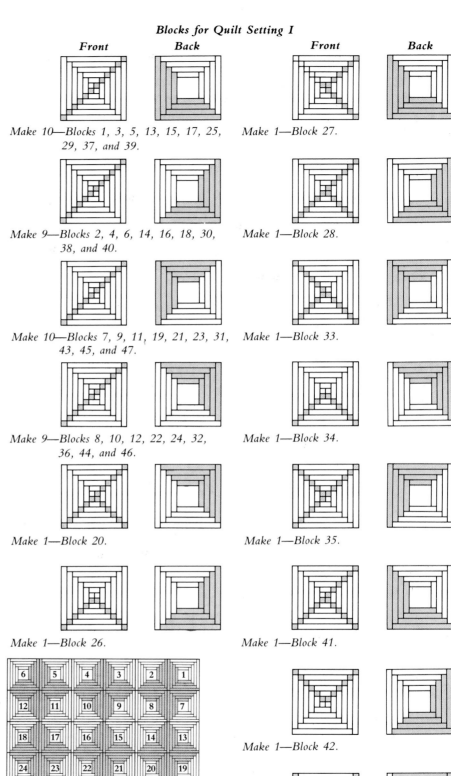

Blocks for Quilt Setting I

Front Back

Make 10—Blocks 1, 3, 5, 13, 15, 17, 25, 29, 37, and 39.

Make 9—Blocks 2, 4, 6, 14, 16, 18, 30, 38, and 40.

Make 10—Blocks 7, 9, 11, 19, 21, 23, 31, 43, 45, and 47.

Make 9—Blocks 8, 10, 12, 22, 24, 32, 36, 44, and 46.

Make 1—Block 20.

Make 1—Block 26.

Front Back

Make 1—Block 27.

Make 1—Block 28.

Make 1—Block 33.

Make 1—Block 34.

Make 1—Block 35.

Make 1—Block 41.

Make 1—Block 42.

Make 1—Block 48.

Back

Quilt Setting II

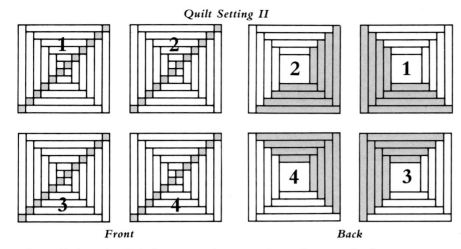

Front   *Back*

Make 12 blocks each. With this setting, there is no design change on the front. Diagonal lines of cornerstones will run down the quilt.

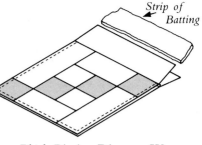

Block Piecing Diagram IV

2. Cut or set aside fabric for 1¼″-wide binding strips from yellow and scrap fabrics before cutting individual block strips.

3. Since Block 1 is the same for both settings, begin with the basic Cornerstone block. Alternate colors of four 1¼″ squares (all measurements for squares and strips include seam allowance) and join to make a larger square. (See Block Piecing Diagrams I.) In log cabin fashion, add one round of 1¼″-wide strips with cornerstones as shown.

Cut a 3½″ square from yellow and from batting. Layer as shown in Block Piecing Diagram II and edgestitch layers together along all four sides. (In these instructions, the Cornerstone block will be on the *front* of the quilt, and the Traditional Spiraling block will be on the *back* of the quilt.)

Continue joining 1¼″ strips and inserting strips of batting in this manner. Refer to the Strip Order Diagram for Front and Back Blocks for the number of strips to add. Notice that, as you sew, the front block will be building counterclockwise and the back block clockwise.

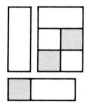

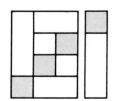

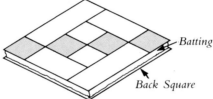

Block Piecing Diagram II

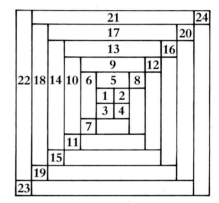

Strip Order Diagram for Front Block

Cut two strips (one scrap strip for the front and one yellow strip for the back), 1¼″ wide. Join to square, as shown in Block Piecing Diagram III. Refer to Block Piecing Diagram IV and insert a strip of batting.

Block Piecing Diagrams I

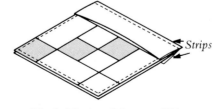

Block Piecing Diagram III

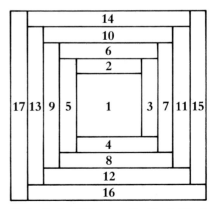

Strip Order Diagram for Back Block

4. Make a total of 48 blocks in this manner for either setting. Refer to Quilt Setting I or II for proper placement of scrap strips and cornerstone squares.

15

5. Arrange blocks in eight rows of six blocks each, as shown in Quilt Setting I or II. Join two Traditional Spiraling blocks, as shown in Row Assembly Diagram I. Press seam to one side. (If using a bulky fabric, some quilters may prefer not to insert any batting at this step.) Overlap Cornerstone block strips, as shown in Row Assembly Diagram II. Blindstitch strip to block.

Join rows in the same manner.

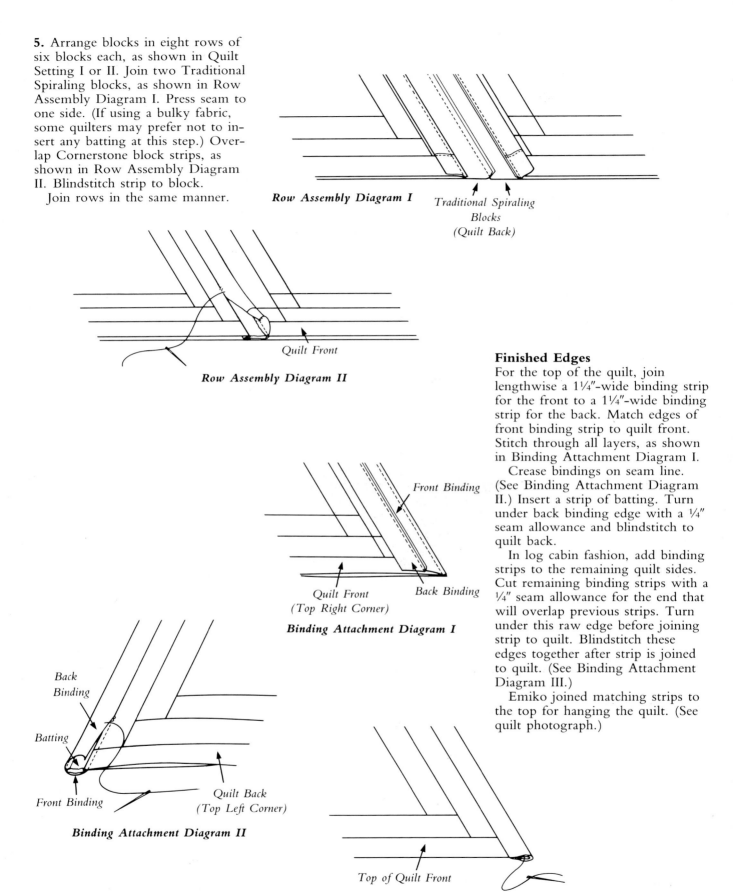

Row Assembly Diagram I

Traditional Spiraling Blocks (Quilt Back)

Quilt Front

Row Assembly Diagram II

Front Binding

Quilt Front (Top Right Corner)

Back Binding

Binding Attachment Diagram I

Back Binding

Batting

Front Binding

Quilt Back (Top Left Corner)

Binding Attachment Diagram II

Top of Quilt Front

Binding Attachment Diagram III

Finished Edges

For the top of the quilt, join lengthwise a 1¼″-wide binding strip for the front to a 1¼″-wide binding strip for the back. Match edges of front binding strip to quilt front. Stitch through all layers, as shown in Binding Attachment Diagram I.

Crease bindings on seam line. (See Binding Attachment Diagram II.) Insert a strip of batting. Turn under back binding edge with a ¼″ seam allowance and blindstitch to quilt back.

In log cabin fashion, add binding strips to the remaining quilt sides. Cut remaining binding strips with a ¼″ seam allowance for the end that will overlap previous strips. Turn under this raw edge before joining strip to quilt. Blindstitch these edges together after strip is joined to quilt. (See Binding Attachment Diagram III.)

Emiko joined matching strips to the top for hanging the quilt. (See quilt photograph.)

Sourdine
1984

Have any old suits that you are ready to give away? Wait and take a look at *Sourdine*. Every piece of *Sourdine* is cut from fabrics used to make men's suits. Emiko was given a large collection of sample swatches from discontinued men's summer suit stock that included lightweight wools and polyester blends.

Musicians of long ago used a sourdine to mute the sounds from their instruments. The muting in this quilt, of course, is not of sound but of color—soft grays, browns, blues, and greens. "These subtle shades were quite a design challenge," admits Emiko. "But it gave me a chance to display my interest in interlocking patterns."

Sourdine

Finished Quilt Size
52" x 68"

Number of Blocks and Finished Size
48 blocks—8" x 8"

Fabric Requirements
Scraps — 7⅓ yd. total
Bias binding — 1¼ yd.
Backing — 3 yd.

Number to Cut
Template A — 192 scraps
Template A★ — 192 scraps
Template B — 384 scraps
Template B★ — 384 scraps
★ — Flip or turn over template if fabric is one-sided.

Quilt Top Assembly
1. Join 2 triangles (B) on long sides, as shown in Block Piecing Diagram. Join them to triangle (A) to complete unit. Make another unit and join units on longest side to form a square. Make 4 squares and join at sides to complete block. Make 48 blocks, alternating fabric patterns and colors, as shown in quilt photograph.

2. Join 6 blocks at sides to form a row. Make 8 rows and join rows.

Quilting
Outline-quilt ¼" inside seam line of triangles (A, B), as shown in Quilting Diagram.

Finished Edges
Bind with bias strips of a matching fabric. Emiko's finished binding width for the front is 1¾". Her bias strips were cut so that she could miter corners.

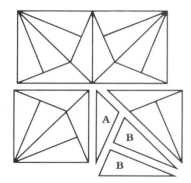

Sourdine *Block Piecing Diagram*

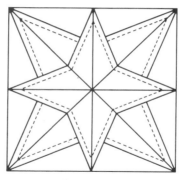

Quilting Diagram

Patsy R. McCoy

Pittsburgh, Pennsylvania

This former kindergarten teacher and transplanted Oklahoman confesses she never had a chance *not* to become an avid quiltmaker. Her mother, grandmother, and other relatives from west Texas were all quilters. She learned to sew at the age of six by making a doll quilt with the help of her grandmother. "My grandmother and mother inspired me to make quilts as they did, from scraps and leftovers from other sewing projects," says Patsy. And still today, Patsy finds that the greatest challenge in quiltmaking is to work out good designs and color usage from existing supplies.

Patsy has been teaching quilting in her home since 1982, and her quilts have been exhibited in over 15 shows in the last three years. "Designing the quilt is my favorite part of quiltmaking," claims Patsy. She finds resources and inspirations for her quilts in the photographs she has taken of interesting designs and/or scenes she observes while traveling with her husband.

Thanks to All My Charming Friends
1986

This classic charm quilt pattern, sometimes known as Spools or Friendship Chain, provides the stage for Patsy to show off her ability to create an eye-catching harmony of colors. Seven hundred and two different fabrics were arranged and rearranged before being sewn together. "I made a rule for myself," says Patsy. "If I could go to my workroom three consecutive times without rearranging the pieces on my pinning board, I could sew them together!" Friends who gave Patsy the fabric for the quilt have autographed the backing behind their pieces to make this a very special quilt for her.

Thanks to All My Charming Friends

Finished Quilt Size
78″ x 83″

Fabric Requirements
Scraps — 8¼ yd. total★
Scraps for border — 1⅝ yd. total
Bias binding — 1¼ yd.
Backing — 4½ yd.
★ — To make a charm quilt from friends' scraps, one 4″ x 5″ rectangle of scrap fabric is all that is needed for one charm.

Number to Cut
Charm — 600 scraps
102 border fabrics

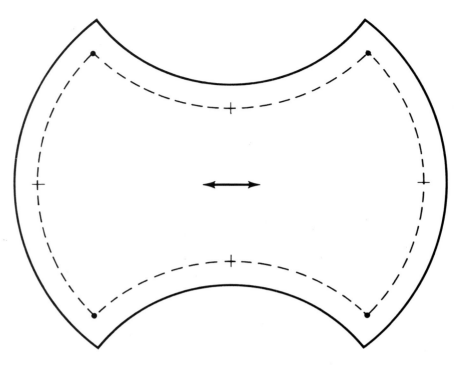

Quilt Top Assembly
1. Alternate 13 vertically placed charms with 13 horizontally placed charms to form a row. (See Assembly Diagram.) Begin and end each row with a charm from border fabric. Patsy found that a large pinning board was helpful for arranging charms before they were sewn. Make 25 rows as above and 2 rows from border fabrics only.

Says Patsy, "I sewed these rows on the machine because I could alternate which part was on the top (the preceding charm or the new one). This allowed me to always have the convex curve next to the feed dogs. But I really think it is best to sew these rows together by hand."

2. Join rows. Patsy recommends hand-piecing the rows together.

Quilting
Refer to Quilting Diagram and outline-quilt ¼″ from charm seam lines across each row. Quilt vertical curved lines that mirror the curved seam lines of the charms, as shown in Quilting Diagram.

Finished Edges
Bind with a continuous bias strip of matching border fabric.

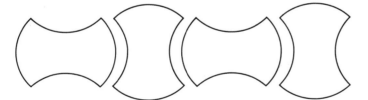

Assembly Diagram

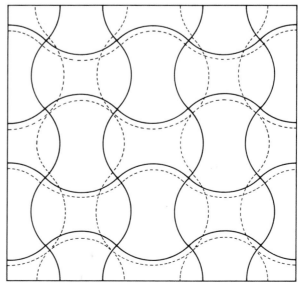

Quilting Diagram

When Janice was a girl, her mother insisted she learn to make a quilt. Janice now confesses, "At the time, I didn't know that there was much more to it than a top. But later while participating in a quilting bee, an older lady taught me, and I was off." Since then, quilting has provided the extra source of income for Janice that is often needed when raising four sons. After her husband died, she entered a few quilt competitions, taught a few library patrons, displayed some of her quilts, gave some away, and set some up in store windows. "Quilting buys that extra gift, wins a needed ribbon for my club, decorates the church wall, and paid and continues to pay many bills. I'm not exaggerating when I admit I couldn't make it without quilting," says Janice.

Janice Ferguson McClung
Lewisburg, West Virginia

Ole Olson to America
1983

Over 150 years ago, 300 passengers left the shores of Europe in a small sailing vessel bound for America. Among them were Janice's Norwegian great-great-grandparents and their four children. After more than seven weeks of sailing the Atlantic, these hopeful Norwegians, named Svenson, arrived in America and discovered that no one could speak Norwegian. And these new settlers couldn't speak English. During the maze of confusion and noise of disembarking, passenger names were hastily recorded. There was no time for interpreters to overcome communication barriers. When the young Svenson family reached the recorder's desk, the recorder believed Mr. Svenson was saying his name was Olson. As Janice tells it, "Since he didn't find out until much later that he was given another name, he kept the name." And since his last name was Olson, he decided his first name should be Ole (pronounced O-lē).

This family story inspired Janice to design *Ole Olson to America*. It was her great-great-grandparents' vision of a bright future for their children in the new land that Janice deemed worthy of honoring. Maybe you have in your background an "Ole Olson" whose revered memory deserves documentation, too.

Ole Olson to America

Finished Quilt Size
Approximately 90" x 100"

Number of Blocks and Finished Size
16 Ship blocks—14½" x 17"

Fabric Requirements
Scraps	—2 yd. total
Solids	— ½ yd. total
Blue print	—5¾ yd.
Blue	—1 yd.
White	—3½ yd.
Blue print for bias binding	—1¼ yd.
Backing	—8 yd.

Embroidery Floss
2 skeins black

Number to Cut
Template A★	—96 scraps
Template B★	—48 scraps
Template C★	—32 scraps
Template D	—16 solids
Template E	—16 blue print
Template F	—16 blue

★ — This is the basic sail shape. Janice suggests cutting these shapes smaller or larger to make each sail look different. Be sure they have one curved edge to suggest billowing sails.

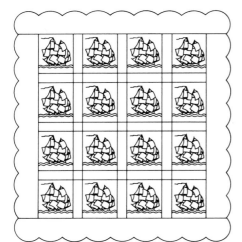

Quilt Top Assembly
1. Cut sixteen 15" squares from white. Layer-appliqué ship (D) and sails (A, B, C) to each white square, as shown in Ship Block Diagram. Clip seam allowances of curved edges to ease appliquéd edge. Layer-appliqué waves (E, F), beginning with wave (E). (*Seam line*

of wave (E) should begin 1" from the bottom edge of white square.)

Embroider ship mast and rigging, using a backstitch, as shown in Ship Block Diagram. Make 16 Ship blocks.

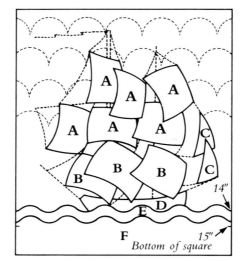

Ship Block Diagram

2. Cut 12 sashing strips, 4½" x 17½", from blue print. Alternate 4 Ship blocks with 3 sashing strips and join at sides to form a row, beginning with a Ship block. Make 4 rows.

3. Cut 12 sashing strips, 4½" x 15", from blue print. Cut nine 4½" accent squares from blue. Alternate 4 sashing strips with 3 accent squares and join to form a sashing row, beginning with a sashing strip. Make 3 sashing rows.

4. Alternate Ship block rows with sashing rows, beginning with a Ship block row. Join rows.

5. Cut 2 border strips, 10½" wide, from blue print for sides and join to quilt.

6. Cut 2 border strips, 10½" wide, from blue print and join to top and bottom of quilt.

7. Use template guideline for scalloped edges to mark border. Match midpoint of template with center of *side* of quilt. Mark along quilt edges and round corners. Leave scalloped edges uncut until quilting is done.

Quilting
Outline-quilt inside seam lines of sails, ship, waves, sashing strips, and accent squares. Refer to Ship Block Diagram for cloud quilting lines. Quilt Janice's anchor in each accent square. Quilt waves of quilting lines on sashing and border strips as Janice did, or choose your favorite nautical symbols for the wide borders.

Finished Edges
With right sides together, sew a continuous bias strip of blue print fabric to quilt top along scallop lines. Ease bias strip on the curves and pivot on the inside curve. Trim all layers to ¼" seam allowance. Miter or tuck inside curves. Fold binding to back and blindstitch in place.

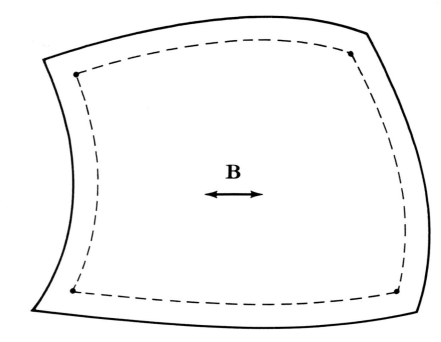

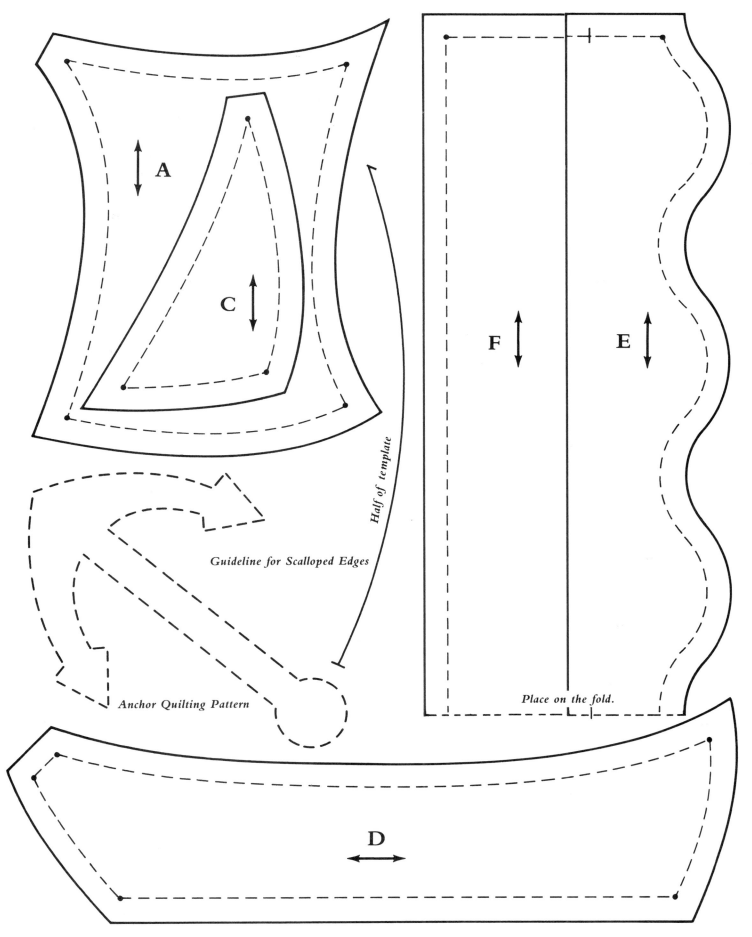

A

C

Half of template

F

E

Guideline for Scalloped Edges

Anchor Quilting Pattern

Place on the fold.

D

Linda Karel Sage

Morgantown, Indiana

By acknowledging the quilters of the past as her role models, Linda has coupled herself with them and defined her commitment to continuing their tradition. "So many women have been making quilts and other needlework over the years under the guise of practical, everyday items," says Linda. "Now we are beginning to realize that a great deal of thought and care went into these creations." And though she thoroughly enjoys developing her own quilt designs, she admits, "I often extract designs from the traditional. One always relies on what has come before as a frame of reference."

Read more about Linda and see her spectacular *Indiana Night Music* in our "Designer Gallery."

Brown County Log Cabins
1985

The Brown County State Park of Indiana, located east of Bloomington, is famous for its log cabin tours. Proud of the beauty and heritage of these log cabins, Linda honors them with their own quilt, *Brown County Log Cabins*.

She carefully selected fabrics to mimic the rustic texture of log cabins and reinforced each cabin's framework with parallel lines of quilting. A lush forest of prairie-point pine trees surrounds Linda's log cabin hamlet.

In 1985 *Brown County Log Cabins* won the Special Judges' Recognition Award for Use of Color at the Mountain Mist Contest. (Linda used Mountain Mist's House Quilt pattern for her log cabins. See "Resources" for details.) In 1986 the quilt won a first place ribbon in the Traditional Patchwork, Amateur category, at the Second Annual American Quilter's Society Show, Best of Show at the Brown County Historical Society's Quilt Show, and first place in the 17th Annual Show of the National Quilting Association.

Brown County Log Cabins

Finished Quilt Size
Approximately 86" x 100"

Number of Blocks and Finished Size
20 Cabin blocks—12" x 12"

Fabric Requirements
Scraps★ of solids, polka
  dots, and stripes — 2½ yd.
               total★★
Stripe   — 2½ yd.
Dk. green   — 2¾ yd.
Med. green   — 1 yd.
Black   — 3½ yd.
Stripe for
  bias binding   — 1¼ yd.
Red for backing — 5½ yd.
★ — Be sure to include a few gold and yellow scraps to suggest lights in cabins.
★★ — Approximate scrap yardage for one cabin is a 16" square.

Number to Cut

Template	Number to Cut
Template A	— 20 black
Template B	— 40 scraps
Template C	— 20 black
Template D	— 20 black
Template E	— 20 scraps
Template F	— 20 black
Template G	— 20 scraps
Template H	— 40 scraps
	40 black
Template I	— 20 scraps
Template J	— 60 scraps
Template K	— 48 scraps
	32 black
Template L	— 16 scraps
	4 black
Template M	— 20 black
Template N	— 180 dk. green
Template O	— 180 med. green

Quilt Top Assembly

1. Linda suggests arranging pieces for each Cabin block before joining. She uses a viewing wall so that she can step back and see the overall effect. Once you are satisfied with each arrangement, join pieces, as shown in Cabin Piecing Diagrams I and II. Make 20 Cabin blocks.

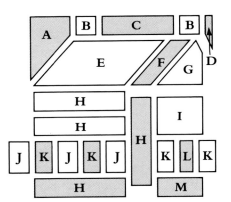

Cabin Piecing Diagram I

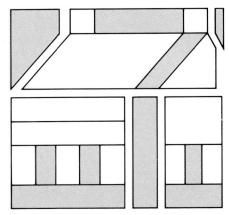

Cabin Piecing Diagram II

2. Cut 16 sashing strips, 4″ wide, from striped fabric. Alternate 5 Cabin blocks with 4 sashing strips and join at tops and bottoms, beginning with a Cabin block to form a vertical row. Intermingle cabins with lights on among those with lights off. (See quilt photograph.) Make 4 vertical rows.

3. Cut 3 sashing strips for the vertical rows, 4″ wide, from striped fabric. Alternate 4 vertical rows with 3 sashing strips and join, beginning with a vertical row.

4. Cut 2 sashing strips, 4″ wide, from striped fabric and join to top and bottom of quilt.

5. Cut 2 sashing strips, 4″ wide, from striped fabric and join to sides of quilt.

6. Cut 2 border strips, 7″ wide, from black and join to top and bottom of quilt.

7. Cut 2 border strips, 7″ wide, from black and join to sides of quilt.

8. Join a continuous bias strip, 1¼″ wide, from striped fabric to quilt.

Quilting

Linda varied her quilting in each Cabin block. Some blocks are quilted with diagonal parallel lines, 1½″ apart, running from "Maine to California," while others have horizontal or crosshatched quilting lines across the cabin. "The idea," says Linda, "is to try for a stacked-log look on the cabins. Experiment with your quilting design to give your cabins that personal touch."

Outline-quilt ¼″ inside seam lines of striped sashing. Quilt parallel waves of quilting, 1¼″ apart, along sashing strips. Quilt the mountain and sunrise pattern on black border strips, placing it so that sunrises meet in the corners to form a half circle. (See Quilting Diagram.) All of Linda's quilting was done in red thread.

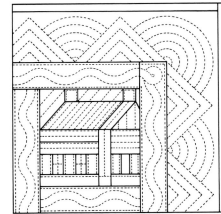

Quilting Diagram

Finished Edges

Fold dark green pine tree points (N and O), as shown in Folding Diagrams and press. To keep points from unfolding, Linda suggests stacking and weighting them until

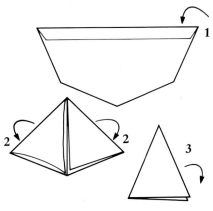

Folding Diagrams

you are ready to use them. Center small pine tree points (O) on large pine tree points (N) and pin. With right sides and raw edges together, stitch 49 pine tree points, side by side, to each side of quilt. Stitch 41 pine tree points, side by side, to the top and 41 to the bottom. (See Pine Tree Points Diagrams I and II.) Turn quilt backing under to cover raw edges of pine tree points and blindstitch in place.

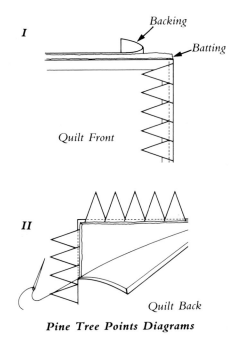

Pine Tree Points Diagrams

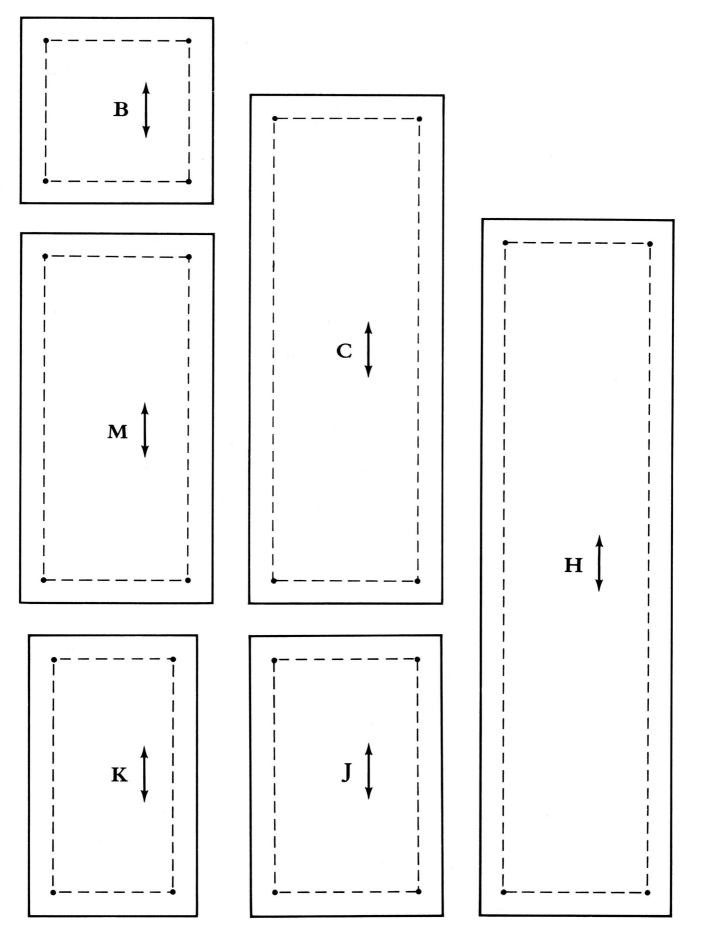

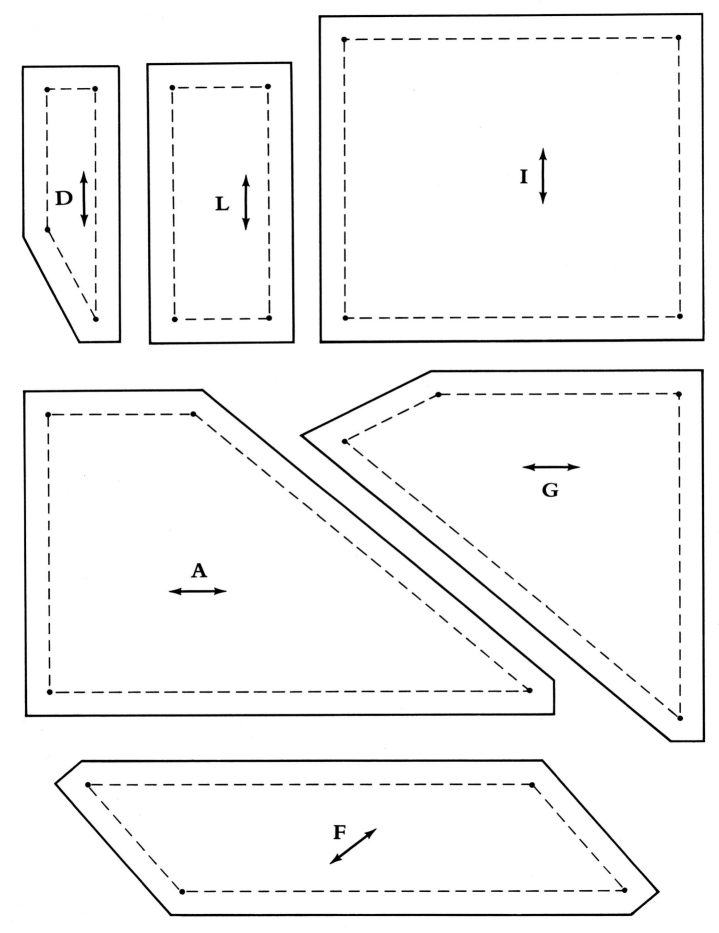

28

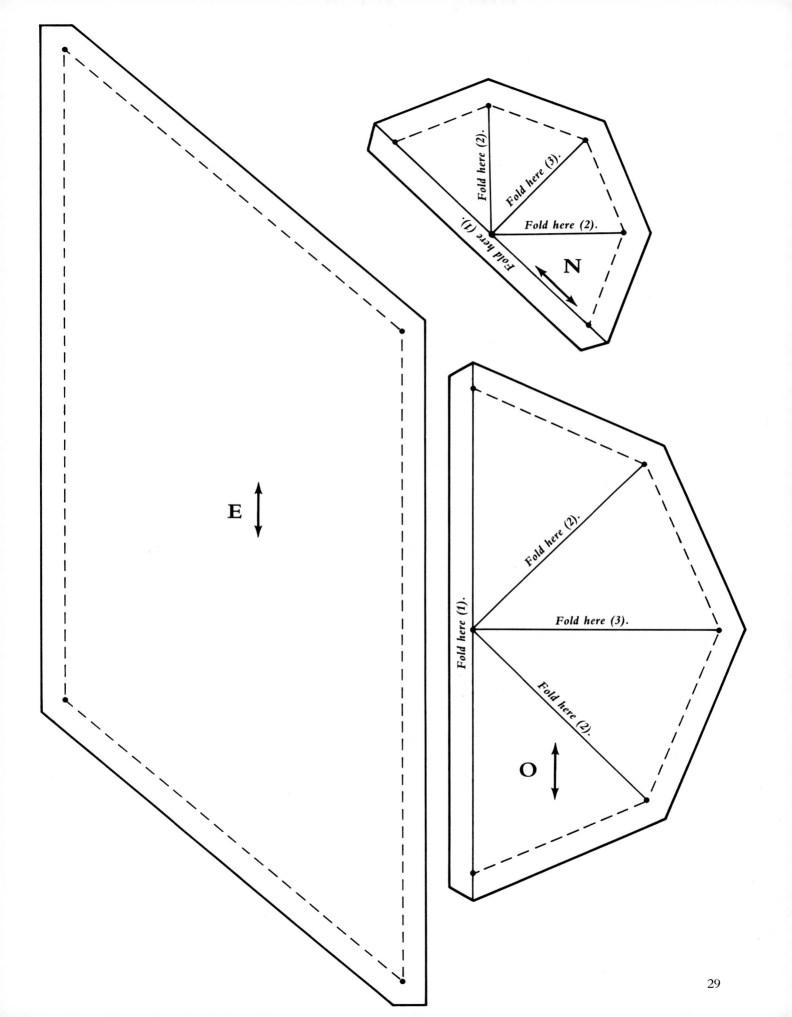

E

Fold here (2).

Fold here (3).

Fold here (2).

Fold here (1).

N

Fold here (1).

Fold here (2).

Fold here (3).

Fold here (2).

O

29

Karen Sikes Collins

Austin, Texas

Unfinished quilts by a mother and a grandmother have brought the most joy and hours of pleasure to this dedicated quilter. "I'm thankful they didn't finish everything," says Karen. "It's a wonderful feeling of sharing an interest with generations past and future." Appropriately, most of her quilting is done sitting on a little couch which she inherited from her great-grandmother, who was also a fine quilter.

Karen learned the basics of quilting by observing her mother, though she doesn't remember her mother ever teaching her. She has made over 50 quilts and prefers pieced ones because they can be sewn anywhere. Says Karen, "Quilting is the one thing that has never let me down. It can calm me down or perk me up. And the more quilting on a quilt, the better I like it."

Scrap Triangles #3
1984

The patterns for a nine-patch scrap quilt are endless, as Karen found out. "The block so fascinated me that I have six quilts in mind, and the fourth is already pieced," says Karen. By sequencing light to dark scrap pieces and turning the blocks, Karen sent ripples of diamonds and pyramids radiating to the quilt's edge. She combined her mother's scraps with her own collection to make *Scrap Triangles #3,* and in a sense, joined generation to generation—past to present.

Scrap Triangles #3

Finished Quilt Size
86″ x 100″

Number of Blocks and Finished Size
168 blocks—7″ x 7″

Fabric Requirements
Scraps   —9 yd. dk.
              colors total
              6 yd. med.
              colors total
              3 yd. lt.
              colors total
Dk. scrap for
  bias binding   —1¼ yd.
Backing   —7½ yd.

Number to Cut
Triangles★   —1,512 dk. colors
            1,008 med. colors
            504 lt. colors
★ — Before cutting, see Quilt Top Assembly, Step 1, for rotary cutter method.

Quilt Top Assembly
1. Cut scrap fabrics into 3″-wide strips, either lengthwise or across the grain. Cut strips into 3″ squares. Cut squares diagonally into two equal triangles until you have cut the required number. Or if you prefer, use triangle template and cut the number of triangles in Number to Cut.
2. Arrange triangles in sets of 9 dark, 6 medium, and 3 light triangles. Sew a dark triangle to a medium or light triangle along bias edge to form squares.

Arrange squares, as shown in Block Piecing Diagram. (Arrow indicates the top of the block.) Join

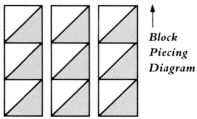

Block Piecing Diagram

31

squares to form columns and join columns to complete block. Make 168 blocks.

3. Arrange 6 blocks into 7 rows, as shown in Block Setting Diagram I for a Quarter of Quilt. Arrows inside blocks indicate the top of each block. The arrow outside the diagram indicates the top of the quarter. Stack rows before assembling. (Karen suggests running a thread through each stack twice to keep the blocks from turning.) Number each stack by row number to help

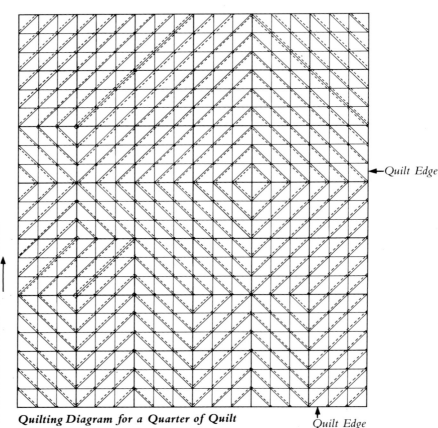

Quilting Diagram for a Quarter of Quilt

←*Quilt Edge*

↑ *Quilt Edge*

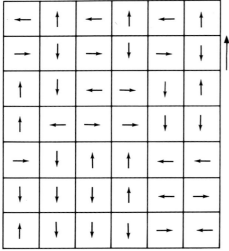

Block Setting Diagram I for a Quarter of Quilt

Block Setting Diagram II for a Quarter of Quilt

with row assembly order. Join blocks at sides to form rows. Join rows to complete a quarter. Trim corners of triangles where bulky on back. Make 4 quarters, with 2 the mirror image of the others. (See Block Setting Diagram II for a Quarter of Quilt.)

4. Join quarters, as shown in Setting Diagram. Arrows indicate the top of each quarter.

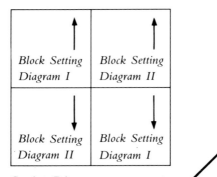

Setting Diagram

Quilting
To reinforce the strong diagonal lines of this quilt, outline-quilt ¼″ inside seam lines of triangles, as shown in Quilting Diagram for a Quarter of Quilt.

Finished Edges
Bind with a continuous bias strip of dark scrap fabric.

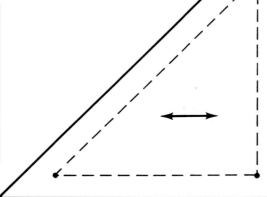

"For as long as I can remember, I've been crazy about fabric," says Alexandra. "I began sewing as a teenager, and it wasn't long before I began to collect fabrics—buying for color and pattern without having an end use in mind."

While studying art in college, Alexandra discovered she loved working with her hands, especially in fiber and clay. "It wasn't until I started quilting that everything seemed to come together," says Alexandra. "With quilting, I have complete control over color, pattern, and design." And best of all, she discovered scrap quilts. "It is a challenge to find homes for all my beloved fabrics," says Alexandra.

Alexandra Pron Gorgol

Haddon Heights, New Jersey

Invisible Stars

1984

Ohio Stars were transformed into *Invisible Stars* by Alexandra's skillful manipulation of fabric hues and patterns. Her process involved drawing the design on graph paper and coloring the Ohio Star blocks so that each star dissolved into the next block. Says Alexandra, "It was an untraditional approach to a traditional pattern." Scraps were sorted into medium and dark colors, and a light print was selected to use as a background fabric for continuity.

This satisfied quilter is still sure that the process was worthwhile, since years later she says contentedly, "Every time I look at *Invisible Stars,* I know that all my choices were good ones."

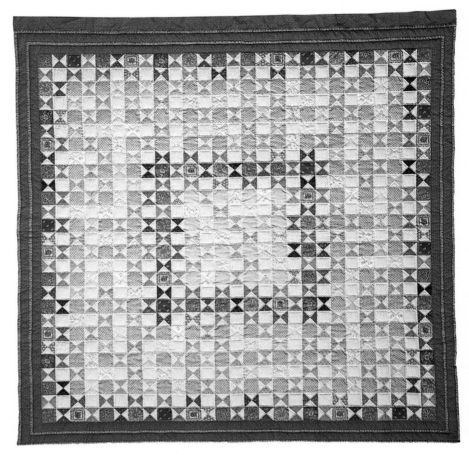

Invisible Stars

Finished Quilt Size
90" x 90"

Number of Blocks and Finished Size
40 block A—9" x 9"
41 block B—9" x 9"

Fabric Requirements
Lt. background print	— 3¾ yd.
Med. scraps	— 2½ yd.
Dk. scraps	— 1⅞ yd.
Border print	— 2¾ yd.
Border stripe and bias binding	— 2¾ yd.
Backing	— 7½ yd.

Number to Cut
Template A	— 169 lt. background print
	124 med. scraps
	72 dk. scraps
Template B	— 728 lt. background print
	408 med. scraps
	320 dk. scraps

Quilt Top Assembly

1. Join squares (A) and triangles (B), as shown in Block A and Block B Piecing Diagrams. Referring to Fabric Color Charts for Blocks A and B, make the number of blocks indicated.

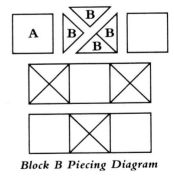

Block B Piecing Diagram

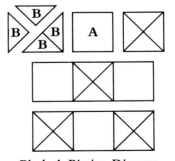

Block A Piecing Diagram

Fabric Color Charts for Block A

Make 24.   Make 12.   Make 4.

Fabric Color Charts for Block B

Make 4.   Make 16.   Make 12.

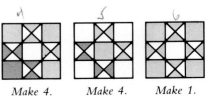

Make 4.   Make 4.   Make 1.

☐ **lt. background print**
▨ **med. scraps**
▦ **dk. scraps**

2. Refer to quilt photograph and arrange blocks in 9 rows of 9 blocks each. Join blocks at sides to form rows. Join rows.

3. Cut 2 border strips, 5″ wide, and join to sides of quilt. Cut 2 border strips, 5″ wide, and join to top and bottom of quilt.

To give the appearance of a striped border fabric, Alexandra appliquéd a stripe along the midpoint of the border width and mitered the corners. (See quilt photograph. This is the same striped fabric she used for binding.)

Quilting

Outline-quilt ¼″ inside seam line of all light background triangles and squares. Outline-quilt ⅛″ inside seam line of border strip. Outline-quilt outside seam line of appliquéd stripe on border.

Finished Edges and Casing

Bind with a continuous bias strip of striped fabric.

Alexandra prefers to hang her quilt and has attached a casing to the top of the quilt. To attach a casing, cut border fabric 8″ wide for top of quilt, leaving a ¼″ seam allowance at each end. Fold under seam allowance on each end and ½″ on each side, and press. Fold casing in half lengthwise, wrong sides together, and machine-edgestitch sides together.

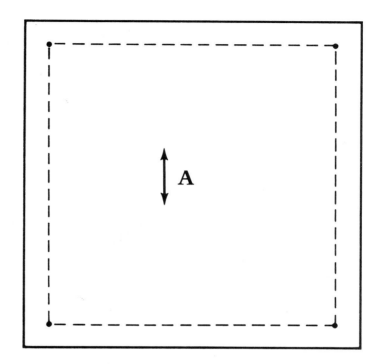

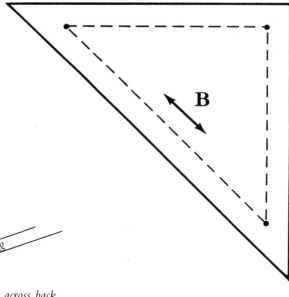

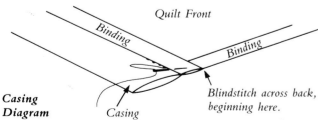

Quilt Front

Binding

Binding

Blindstitch across back, beginning here.

Casing Diagram

Casing

Follow with a second row of stitching ¼″ from edgestitching for reinforcement. Place casing under quilt binding and blindstitch to quilt back only. (See Casing Diagram.) Blindstitch binding to casing.

Tora Sterregaard
Phoenix, Arizona

When the scrap bag is bulging, Tora takes root in front of her sewing machine and, in a whirl of spontaneity, begins strip-piecing snatches of fabric as she pulls them out of the bag. "I prefer this method," explains Tora, "because colors fall together that I might have never planned. Sometimes I have a block pattern in mind, and sometimes not." But at this stage, color playing against color is the most important factor for Tora.

Another color game Tora often plays is the "balls of yarn toss." By pouring several different-colored balls of yarn out of a cylinder, she can study the resulting color combinations and choose her next color scheme from them. "Just as in spontaneous strip-piecing, I discover color relationships that I might have never tried," says Tora.

Be sure to turn to the "Quilts Across America" chapter to view more of Tora's expert handling of color.

Indian Spiral
1986

Every quilter has an ample resource of scraps, and Tora confesses, "I have two scrap bags. One is full of small chunks of fabric, and one has strips of any size." Her strips and chunks are salvaged from quilt projects, from the long wedges left from straightening the grain, and from clothing projects.

Indian Spiral is Tora's scrap rendition of the Indian Hatchet block. For the best results she recommends, "Quilters should make sure their scraps are a good variety of dark, medium, and light colors, and select one or two strips of bright red and bright yellow to act as seasoning to the stew."

Indian Spiral

Finished Quilt Size
Approximately 91" x 91"

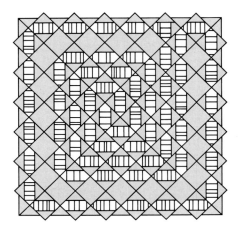

Number of Blocks and Finished Size
65 pieced blocks—9" x 9"

Fabric Requirements
Scrap fabrics — 3¼ yd. total
Rust — 4¼ yd.
Black — ¾ yd.
Black for bias
  binding — 1¼ yd.
Backing — 8 yd.

Number to Cut
Template A — 129 rust
  28 black
Template B — 64 strip-pieced
  scraps
Template C — 1 rust
Template D — 1 rust
Template E — 2 strip-pieced
  scraps
Template F — 1 strip-pieced
  scraps

Quilt Top Assembly

1. Sew strips of scrap fabrics together lengthwise to make large pieces. Tora suggests grouping strips of similar lengths together and varying the widths and color values as you sew. Cut the required number of templates B, E, and F, shifting shapes to avoid identical strip arrangements. (See Strip-Pieced Template Layout.) Sew unused sections together to make new strip-pieces.

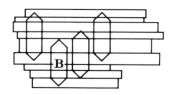

Strip-Pieced Template Layout

2. Join 2 rust triangles (A) to 1 strip-pieced (B), as shown in Block Piecing Diagram I. Make 64 blocks.

Block Piecing Diagram I

3. Join strip-pieced shapes (E and F) to rust shapes (A, C, and D), as shown in Block Piecing Diagram II. Make 1 block.

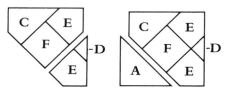

Block Piecing Diagram II

4. Cut nineteen 9½″ squares from rust. Arrange squares with strip-pieced blocks, as shown in Setting Diagram. Join blocks at sides to form rows, attaching black triangles at the ends of each row as shown. Join rows.

5. Join 2 black triangles (A) at sides for corner piece. Make 4 and attach to quilt. (See Setting Diagram.)

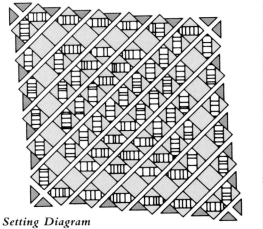

Setting Diagram

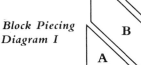

Quilt Edge

Quilting Diagram

Quilting

Quilt straight lines across strip-pieced shape (B), 1″ inside seam lines, and continue across the adjacent block, as shown in Quilting Diagram. Refer to Quilting Diagram and complete block with Tora's quilting design for corner triangles. Quilt this same design in each corner of rust squares, as shown in Quilting Diagram.

Finished Edges

Make a continuous bias strip, 2½″ wide, from black fabric. Press in half lengthwise (wrong sides together) to make a double or French binding. Make mitered tucks at all convex corners and stretch binding slightly at all concave corners. Fold binding to back and blindstitch in place.

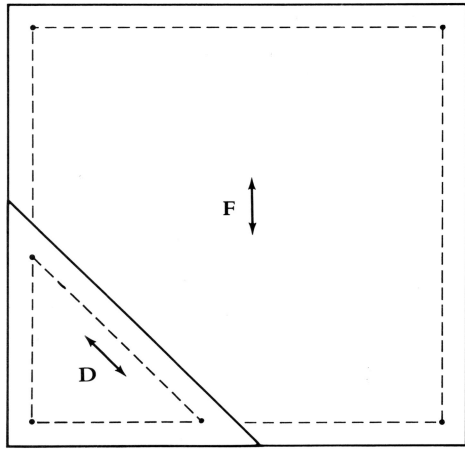

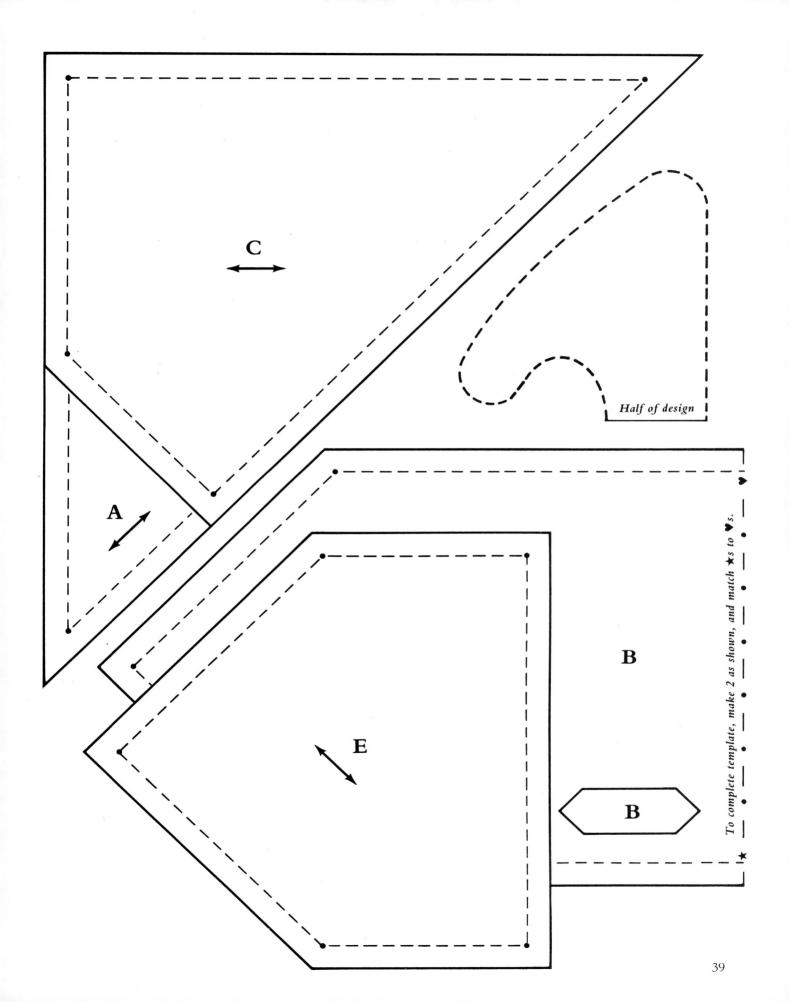

C

Half of design

A

E

B

B

To complete template, make 2 as shown, and match ★s to ♥s.

QUILTS ACROSS AMERICA

A quilt speaks to its maker. . .

I look up into your eyes. I see care, love, and determination.
  I see inspiration and enthusiasm. I see my reflection.
Sometimes I see frustration, but not for long.
  And again I feel safe in your care.
Your eyes sparkle as your stitches work, in a sound I've grown accustomed
  to—punch and pop, whisk and tug, squeeze and pinch.

Suddenly, the sound stops.
Satisfaction radiates from your eyes. Do I see a tear?
You've done so much for me; it's my turn to shine for you.
Now I'm free to nestle against the meandering boundaries
  you purposely established.
I'll miss being near you, knowing your joys and displeasures.
But, just the daily sweep of your hand across my dimpled surface assures me
  I am not forgotten.

Irish Apple
1983

Mix 25 freshly picked and scrumptiously red apples with a handsome Irish Chain, and you have the *Irish Apple*. Strip-pieced in "apple"-pealing hues of red, green, and blue, the quilt preserves the charm of the apple orchard for all to share.

And while you're busy appliquéing apples, don't be surprised if you have a sudden craving for a nibble of that crunchy fruit. Just look what happened to one of Gloria's polished gems!

Gloria Brown
Tulsa, Oklahoma

Self-actualization is the word that best describes the feeling Gloria receives from her quilting. "Quilting and quilt-related activities provide a certain continuity in my life," says Gloria. "It is the one thing I do for myself." Gloria especially enjoys the new friendships produced by the common ground of quilting. "I sometimes tell people that I am a member of a worldwide underground network of women who hoard scraps of fabric!" chuckles Gloria.

Her quilting expertise is readily shared in her roles as teacher, writer, and lecturer. "It thrills me to show individuals how to quilt and then see them reach their goal," says Gloria. "Making a quilt is a lofty project, and I have seen many women gain a deep sense of self-worth by making one." Gloria has served as the President, Vice President, and Educational Chairman of her local guild and was recently elected President of the Oklahoma Quilters State Organization. And all of this from a person who made her first quilt in 1970, using an old beach towel for batting.

Irish Apple

Finished Quilt Size
78" x 78"

Number of Blocks and Finished Size
24 Apple blocks—10" x 10"
1 Apple Core block—10" x 10"
24 Irish Chain blocks—10" x 10"

Number to Cut
Template A — 24 red
Template B — 1 red
Template C — 25 green
Template D — 25 brown

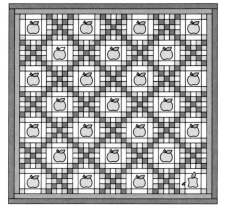

Fabric Requirements
Red with white
  pin dots★   —2½ yd.
Green with white
  pin dots★   —2¼ yd.
Navy   —4½ yd.
Brown   — ⅛ yd.
White   —2¾ yd.
Navy for bias
  binding   —1¼ yd.
Backing   —4½ yd.
★ — Throughout the directions, red with white pin dots and green with white pin dots will be designated red and green, respectively.

Quilt Top Assembly
1. Cut strips, 2½" wide, *across* fabric as follows: 25—red, 14—navy, and 17—white. (Set aside 6 red strips and 10 white strips for making combination strips D and E in Step 5.)

2. Referring to Combination Strip Diagrams, sew combination strips as follows:

Combination Strip A (make 3): navy, red, white, red, navy

Combination Strip B (make 3): red, navy, red, navy, red

Combination Strip C (make 2): white, red, navy, red, white

3. Before cutting combination strips, press all seams to the darker side. Cut strips, 2½″ wide, across seam lines of combination strips as follows:

48 from Combination Strip A
48 from Combination Strip B
24 from Combination Strip C

4. Join 2½″-wide combination strips at sides in following order to form one block: A, B, C, B, A. (See Block Piecing Diagram I.) Make 24 blocks.

5. Cut 8 strips, 6½″ wide, *across* the fabric from white. Referring to Combination Strip Diagrams, sew combination strips D and E with a 6½″-wide strip in the center and 2½″-wide strips on sides as follows:

Combination Strip D (make 3): red, white, red

Combination Strip E (make 4): white, white, white

6. Cut fifty strips, 2½″ wide, across seam lines of Combination Strip D. Cut twenty-five strips, 6½″ wide, across seam lines of Combination Strip E.

Combination Strip Diagrams

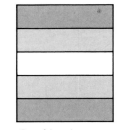

Combination Strip A

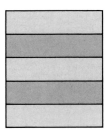

Combination Strip B

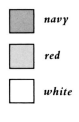

Combination Strip C

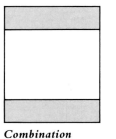

Combination Strip D

Combination Strip E

navy
red
white

7. Join strips at sides in following order: D, E, D. (See Block Piecing Diagram II.) Make 25 blocks.

8. Appliqué 24 blocks with whole apples (A) and 1 block with apple core (B). Appliqué stem first; then apple and leaf. See quilt drawing for position of stem and leaf of core.

9. Alternate 4 Apple blocks with 3 pieced blocks and join at sides, beginning with an Apple block to form a row. Make 4 rows. *Remember to decide where you want to place your Apple Core block before joining rows.*

10. Alternate 4 pieced blocks with 3 Apple blocks and join at sides, beginning with a pieced block to form a row. Make 3 rows.

11. Alternate rows made in Steps 9 and 10 and join.

12. Cut border strips, 2½″ wide, from green. Join to sides first and then to top and bottom.

13. Cut border strips, 2½″ wide, from navy. Join to sides first and then to top and bottom.

Quilting

Outline-quilt outside appliqué seam edge. The remainder of the quilt is quilted with a 1½″ cross-hatching pattern.

Finished Edges

Bind with a continuous bias strip of navy fabric.

Block Piecing Diagram I

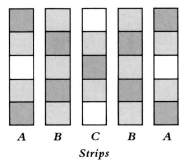

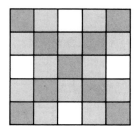

A B C B A

Strips

Block Piecing Diagram II

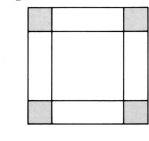

Strips   D   E   D

44

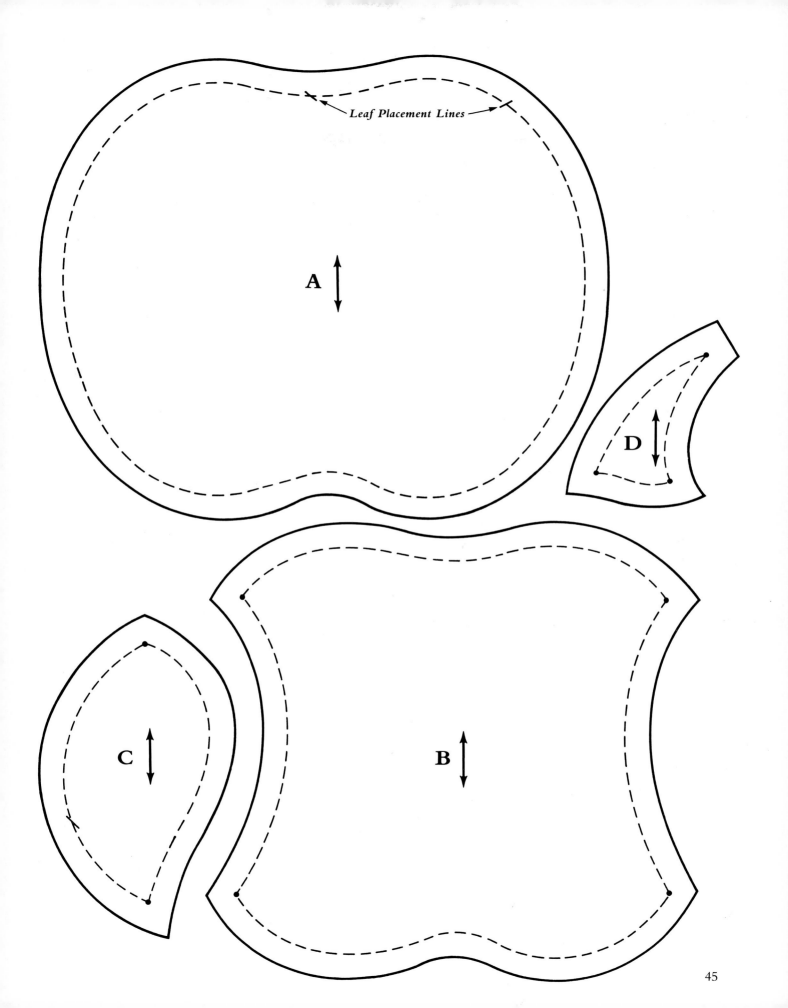

Leaf Placement Lines

A

D

C

B

45

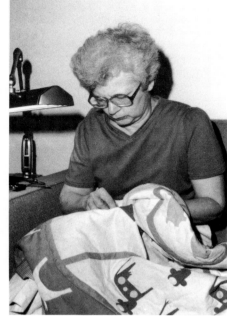

Hallie H. O'Kelley
Tuscaloosa, Alabama

This designer and printer of greeting cards has combined her artistic talents with her sewing talents for quiltmaking purposes. Quiltmaking was something Hallie had in mind to try someday when she had lots of free time. But when the idea struck her to plan a quilt for which she could print the design, she discovered that quiltmaking encompassed a multitude of creative pleasures. That was six years ago. Today, she averages quilting 30 to 40 hours a week and continues to find the completion of each piece exciting. "Best of all," exults Hallie, "since my husband retired two years ago, he has become a quilter. So quilting has turned out to be an interest which we both can share."

Tulip Garden
1983

The rhythmic sway of newborn blossoms in Hallie's *Tulip Garden* seems to announce the advent of spring. Adapted from one of her own tulip designs for note cards, subtle shades of pink are captured by her screen-printing expertise. By using the technique of screen printing on fabric, Hallie can get both the color and design she wants. "I use screen printing, not as a substitute for an appliquéd design, but rather to achieve fabric colors and designs that are my own and couldn't be achieved any other way," says Hallie.

Patterns and instructions for our purposes are given for appliquéd tulips. But if screen printing is your cup of tea, trim seam allowances from patterns and refer to Placement Diagram. (See "Resources" for a list of instructional materials on screen printing.)

Tulip Garden

Finished Quilt Size
73″ x 90″

Number of Blocks and Finished Size
15 blocks—16¼″ x 12″

Fabric Requirements

Muslin	—5½ yd.
Pink	—1 yd.
Dk. rose	—1¼ yd.
Green	—2½ yd.
Muslin for bias binding	—1¼ yd.
Backing	—5¼ yd.

Number to Cut

Template A	—15 pink
Template B	—30 pink
Template C	—15 pink
Template D	—15 dk. rose
Template E	—15 dk. rose
Template F	—15 dk. rose
Template G	—15 dk. rose
Template H	—15 dk. rose
Template I	—71 pink
	71 dk. rose
	70 green
Template J	—15 green
Template K	—15 green
Template L	—15 green
Template M	—15 green
Template N	—15 green
Template O	—15 green
Template P	—15 green
Template Q	—15 green
Template R	—15 green

Quilt Top Assembly

1. Cut 15 blocks, 16¾″ x 12½″, from muslin. Finger-crease each block in half twice to find the center, for placement of middle tulip. Pin 3 tulips with leaves to muslin block, as shown in Placement Diagram, and appliqué. Appliqué 15 blocks. To aid in appliquéing tulips and leaves, machine-stitch on seam line before turning fabric under.

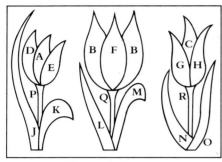

Placement Diagram

2. Cut 18 sashing strips, 3½″ x 16¾″, from muslin. Appliqué 6 tulips (I), side by side, to each sashing strip, alternating colors, as shown in quilt photograph.
3. Alternate 6 sashing strips with 5 appliquéd blocks and join to form a vertical row. Make 3 rows.
4. For vertical rows, cut 4 sashing strips, 3½″ wide, from muslin. Appliqué 26 tulips (I) to each sashing strip, alternating colors, as shown in quilt photograph.
5. Alternate sashing strips with rows and join.
6. Cut 2 border strips, 6½″ wide, from muslin and join to sides of quilt.
7. Cut 2 border strips, 6½″ wide, from muslin and join to top and bottom of quilt.

Quilting Diagram

Quilting

Quilt tulips, as shown in Quilting Diagram. Outline-quilt outside seam lines of sashing tulips. Set off sashing tulips by quilting vertical lines midway between tulips to form a block configuration. (See quilt photograph.) Quilt the remainder of the quilt in parallel horizontal lines 1″ apart.

Finished Edges

Bind with a continuous bias strip of muslin.

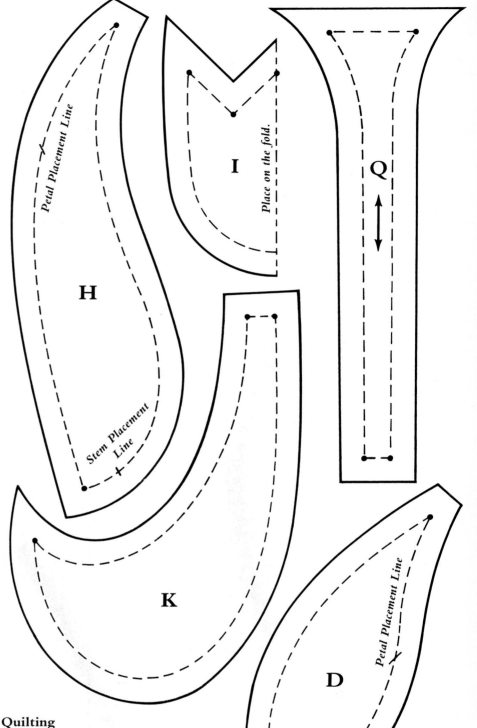

48

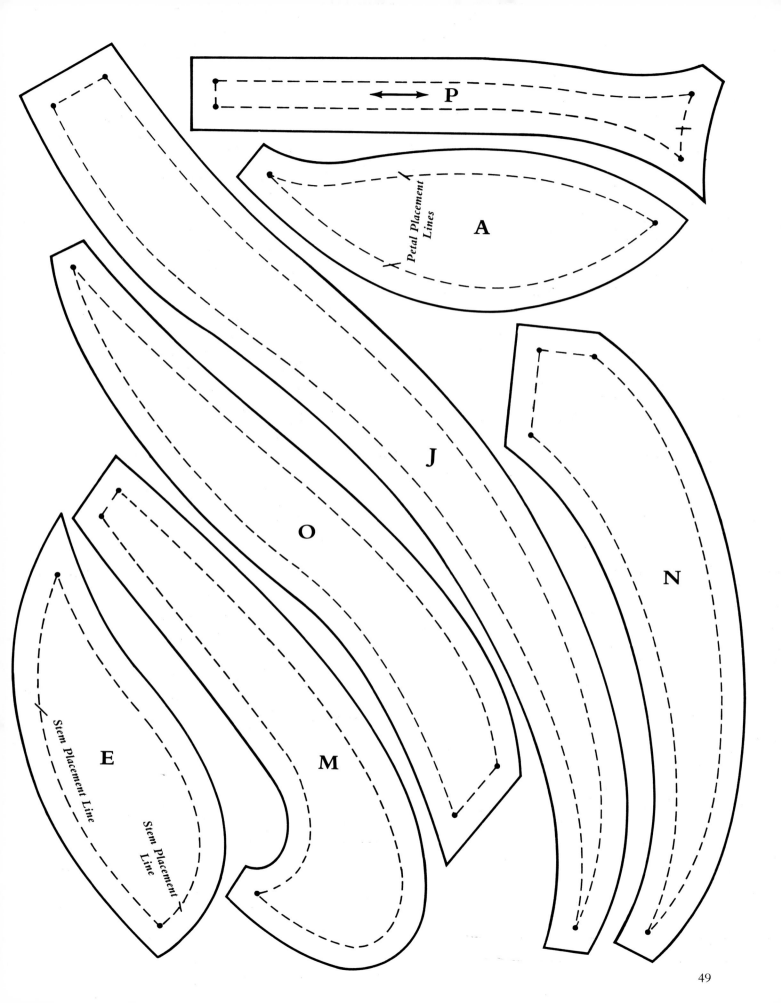

P

A

Petal Placement Lines

J

N

O

E

Stem Placement Line

Stem Placement Line

M

49

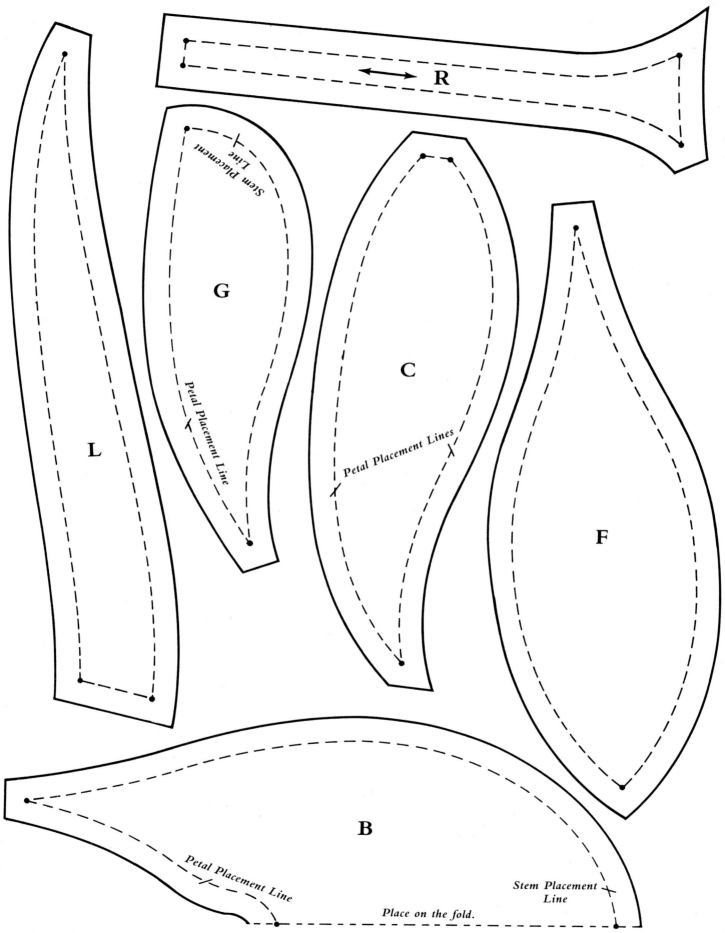

R

Stem Placement Line

G

Petal Placement Line

L

C

Petal Placement Lines

F

B

Petal Placement Line

Stem Placement
Line

Place on the fold.

50

The focus of Elaine's quilting is the interconnectedness she feels with the women who have gone before, and those to come. It is best expressed in the color and pattern selections of her quilts—bold yet soft, unified yet distinct, and traditional yet contemporary. Elaine readily acknowledges that this contrasting and blending are the most important parts of her work.

In much the same light, Elaine discovers a contrast in her emotions when she quilts. "Quilting soothes and excites me at the same time," says Elaine. "My quilts reflect that part of me which needs corners to meet and edges bound. But I always try to inject a freer image—odd color combinations, unexpected fabric types, or delicate details on a bold design."

Elaine Anne Spence

West Linn, Oregon

Double Wedding Ring
1984

Elaine's *Double Wedding Ring* quilt offers us a contemporary twist to a traditional pattern. It was her first hand-quilted project and her first attempt at curved piecing.

The main inspiration for the colors and fine detailing was the love she has for her husband. "They are symbolic to me of our relationship," says Elaine.

Double Wedding Ring

Finished Quilt Size
Approximately 72″ x 94″

Fabric Requirements
Rose pink — ¾ yd.
Charcoal gray — 5½ yd.
Black print — ¾ yd.
Scrap prints — 5½ yd. total
Gray print for
 bias binding — 1¼ yd.
Backing — 5½ yd.

Number to Cut
Template A — 880 scrap prints
Template B — 220 scrap prints
Template B★ — 220 scrap prints
Template C — 122 rose pink
       122 black print
Template D — 48 charcoal gray
Template E — 110 charcoal gray
★ — Flip or turn over template if
fabric is one-sided.

Quilt Top Assembly
1. Select sequence of scrap prints for arc and join sides of 4 arc pieces (A), as shown in Piecing Diagram I. Join an arc piece (B) to each end. Make 2 arcs.

Join a rose square (C) to the ends of one arc, as shown in Piecing Diagram II.

Piecing Diagram I

Piecing Diagram II

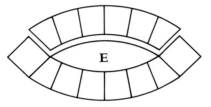

Piecing Diagram III

With right sides together, match the center seam of the arc with the midpoint of shape (E). Join arc to shape (E), beginning and ending stitches *at the seam line,* rather than the fabric edge. In the same manner, join second arc to opposite side of shape (E) and join sides of arc pieces (B) to squares (C) to complete oval, as shown in Piecing Diagram III.

Make 54 ovals with rose squares (C) and 56 ovals with black print squares (C).

2. Referring to quilt photograph, alternate 7 ovals with black print squares with 6 center pieces (D). With right sides together, match the center seam of oval with the midpoint of center piece. As before, begin and end all stitching at the *seam line.* Join ovals and center pieces at sides.

In same manner, join 6 ovals with rose squares to bottom of center pieces to complete a row. (See Row Piecing Diagram.) Make 8 rows. Join rows.

Join 6 ovals with rose squares to top of quilt.

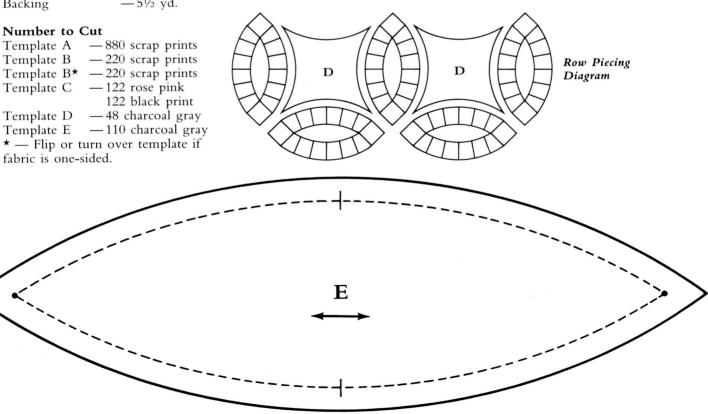

Row Piecing Diagram

E

3. Set a rose square (C) between black print squares at ends of horizontal rows. With right sides together, stitch from outside edge to seam line. Stop and backstitch 1 or 2 stitches. Remove fabric from machine. Align the remaining sides and stitch from the center to the outside edge, backstitching 1 or 2 stitches at the start. Join 14 rose squares to quilt sides and 10 black print squares to top and bottom of quilt.

Quilting
Quilt star-and-heart motif in center pieces (D). Quilt a heart in each square (C) and two hearts in shape (E). (See quilt photograph.)

Finished Edges
Bind with a continuous bias strip of gray print fabric. Ease bias strip and pivot on inside and outside corners. Miter or tuck corners. Fold binding to back and blindstitch in place.

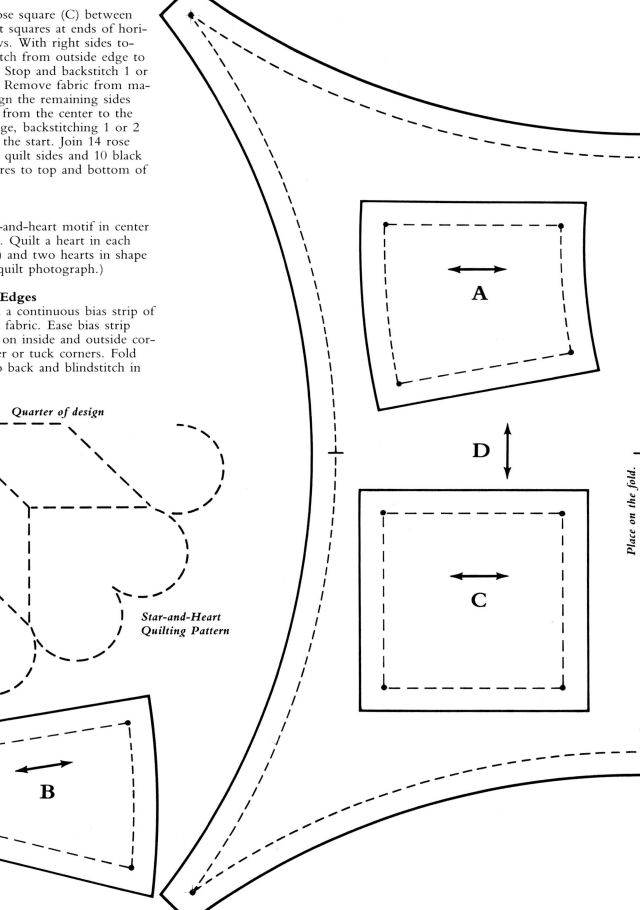

Quarter of design

Star-and-Heart Quilting Pattern

A

D

C

B

Place on the fold.

53

This *Pinwheel* becomes a color wheel of shades from pink to burgundy. "I wanted to experiment with shading in this quilt, and pink and gray are one of my favorite color combinations," says Elaine. *Pinwheel* won a blue ribbon at the Oregon State Fair in 1985.

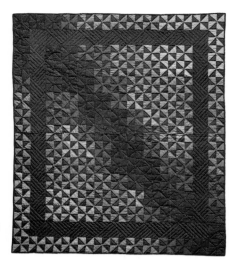

Pinwheel

Finished Quilt Size
78″ x 90″

Number of Blocks and Finished Size
151 blocks—6″ x 6″

Fabric Requirements
Gray	— 4¾ yd.
Burgundy	— ½ yd.
Burgundy, polished cotton	— ¼ yd.
Dark red	— ⅛ yd.
Red	— ¼ yd.
Mauve	— ¼ yd.
Coral	— ½ yd.
Light rose	— ⅝ yd.
Bright pink	— ¼ yd.
Medium peach	— ¼ yd.
Tan	— ¾ yd.
Light peach	— ¼ yd.
Pink	— ⅝ yd.
Burgundy for bias binding	— 1¼ yd.
Backing	— 5¼ yd.

Number to Cut★
Triangle	— 604 gray
	90 burgundy
	20 burgundy, polished cotton
	10 dark red
	40 red
	40 mauve
	64 coral
	76 light rose
	24 bright pink
	26 medium peach
	108 tan
	30 light peach
	76 pink

★ — Some quilters may prefer the quick machine-piecing method for pieced squares. See Step 1.

Quilt Top Assembly

1. Join 4 gray triangles to 4 non-gray triangles to form 4 squares. Join sides of squares to form Pinwheel block, as shown in Block Piecing Diagram. Refer to chart below for number of blocks to make per color. To save time, string-piece all gray triangles with all non-gray triangles and use as needed. Make a total of 151 Pinwheel blocks.

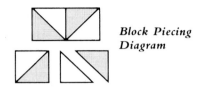

Block Piecing Diagram

Number of Pinwheel Blocks by Color with Gray
Burgundy	— 22
Burgundy, polished cotton	— 5
Dark red	— 2
Red	— 10
Mauve	— 10
Coral	— 16
Light rose	— 19
Bright pink	— 6
Medium peach	— 6
Tan	— 27
Light peach	— 7
Pink	— 19
Burgundy/dark red★★	— 1
Medium peach/light peach★★	— 1

★★ — Use 2 triangles of each color.

If you prefer to use the quick machine-piecing method for pieced squares, lay two fabric rectangles of equal size together. A gray rectangle should always be on the bottom. Mark a grid of 4″ squares on the top fabric. Draw a diagonal line through each square. Machine-stitch ¼″ on either side of diagonal lines. (See Pieced Squares Diagram.) Cut along marked lines. *Before using this method, mark off an area of gray fabric for your one-piece border strips.* (See quilt photograph and Step 3.)

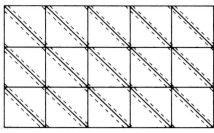

Pieced Squares Diagram

2. Refer to quilt photograph for proper color arrangement and join 9 blocks at sides to form a row. Make 11 rows and join rows.
3. Cut 4 border strips, 6½″ wide, from gray. Join to sides first and then to top and bottom of quilt.
4. Refer to quilt photograph for proper color arrangement and join 13 blocks at sides to make a border strip. Make 4 border strips. Join strips to sides first and then to top and bottom of quilt.

Quilting
Outline-quilt ¼″ inside seam lines of all gray triangles. Quilt striated triangles, as shown in Quilting Diagram for Border Strips. Parallel lines inside triangles are 1″ apart.

Finished Edges
Bind with a continuous bias strip of burgundy fabric.

Quilting Diagram for Border Strips

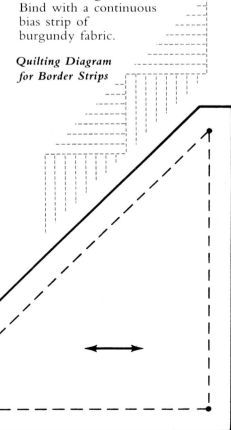

Ami Simms

Flint, Michigan

This enthusiastic quilter claims, "I live in a padded house." Says Ami, "I ran out of beds years ago. Now, I just hang the quilts on the wall." In the last 10 years, Ami has achieved status in the quilting realm as an accomplished quiltmaker, teacher, workshop leader, writer, lecturer, and judge. While she was conducting research for a thesis in anthropology, an Amish woman painstakingly introduced her to quilting. "She patiently guided me through my first quilt and encouraged me in spite of myself," declares Ami.

Today, Ami claims, "I could cheerfully eat, sleep, and breathe quilts. It is the perfect medium." She continues, "I can't envision my life without quiltmaking being a part of it. The challenge never ends." Enjoy Ami's *La Strada* and *Neuschwanstein* in our "Designer Gallery."

Whig Rose
1984

Ami admits *Whig Rose* represents a big chunk of her life. But she says, "Long-term commitment, lasting value, and endurance are virtues that don't get much exercise these days." According to Ami, the time spent making quilts can be a lasting record of activities, thoughts, and feelings. "Like songs we hear on the radio that conjure strong memories of a particular time and place, quilts help us recall that part of life that is sewn up into them," explains Ami.

Special memories abound within *Whig Rose* for Ami. "We applied to adopt a child, had our home study, received our assignment, greeted our Korean daughter at the airport, and lost her maternal grandfather to cancer," remembers Ami. This quilt embodies a very real part of herself.

She drafted the block design from a postcard of a 19th-century variation of the Whig Rose pattern and complemented it with an alluring serpentine border of roses. Even though *Whig Rose* appears to use yards of bias strips, Ami recommends cutting stems and vines using templates. "That way I can be sure the fabric will go where I want it," says Ami.

Whig Rose

Finished Quilt Size
79" x 79"

**Number of Blocks and
Finished Size**
9 blocks—17" x 17"

Fabric Requirements

Red	— ⅝ yd.
Red print	— ¾ yd.
Navy	— ⅛ yd.
Navy print	— ¾ yd.
Green	— 4 yd.
White	— 6 yd.
Red for bias binding	— 1¼ yd.
Backing	— 4⅝ yd.

Number to Cut

Template A	— 28 red print
Template B	— 68 navy print
Template C	— 68 red
Template D	— 292 green
Template E	— 52 red
Template F	— 13 navy
Template G	— 20 green
Template H	— 20 green
Template I	— 20 green
Template J	— 12 green
Template J★	— 12 green
Templates K, L, M	— 8 green vines★★
Template N	— 4 green
Template N★	— 4 green

★ — Flip or turn over template if fabric is one-sided.

★★ — Match ends of templates K, L, M for one complete vine. See Template Placement Diagram for One-piece Vine.

Quilt Top Assembly

1. Cut nine 17½" squares from white. Finger-crease each square on the diagonal; then finger-crease again on the opposite diagonal to find center and to form guidelines for appliqué. Appliqué 5 squares with flowers and stems, as shown in Whig Rose Placement Diagram.

Whig Rose Placement Diagram

For the remaining 4 squares, place a flower (B) with center (C) and 2 leaves (D) in each corner. Place flower petals (E) and circle (F) in the center, as shown in quilt photograph, and appliqué.

Ami's appliqué is neat and precise because of the invisible appliqué stitch she uses. (See "Resources.") To use this type of appliqué stitch, mark placement lines on background fabric and seam lines of appliqué piece before stitching. Lay piece to be appliquéd on top of the background fabric so that sewing lines of background can be seen. Clip seam allowances of any concave curves to about 1/16" from the seam line. Do this just prior to appliquéing to prevent fraying. Begin stitch at a corner, at the end of a bias strip, or, in the case of curved pieces, at an orientation mark. With your needle, pierce the piece to be appliquéd on the seam line from the wrong side, so that your needle exits on the right side. (See Appliqué Stitching Diagram I.) Working from the right side, and moving from right to left, take one small stitch in the background fabric. The stitch should exit on the sewing line one stitch-length away. (See Appliqué Stitching Diagrams II and III.) Insert the needle in appliqué piece at a point exactly opposite the place where the thread exited the fabric from the last stitch. Make a total of

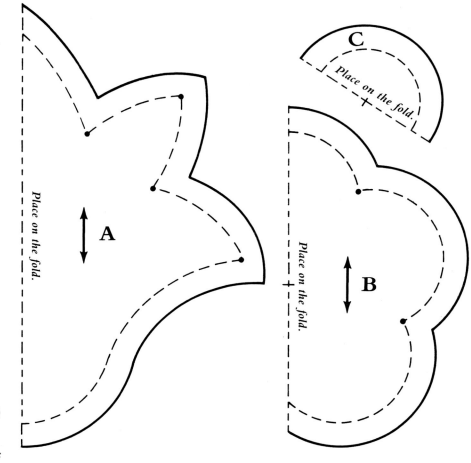

6 stitches. Now gently turn under the seam allowance and pull the thread taut. The thread should disappear, and the appliqué piece lie perfectly flat. Continue stitching in this manner for entire piece.

2. Referring to quilt photograph for proper placement, join appliquéd squares at sides in 3 rows of 3 squares each. Join rows to complete center section.

3. Cut 4 border strips, 14½" wide, from white. Referring to Border Placement Diagram, pin vines and leaves in place and appliqué. Appliqué flowers. Join strips to center section and miter corners. Appliqué center piece (F) to corner flowers.

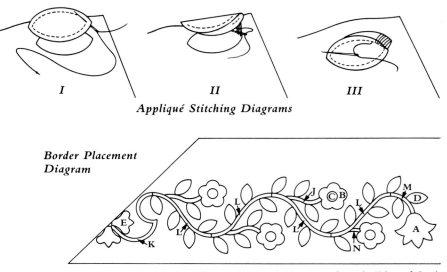

Appliqué Stitching Diagrams

Border Placement Diagram

Outside Edge of Quilt

58

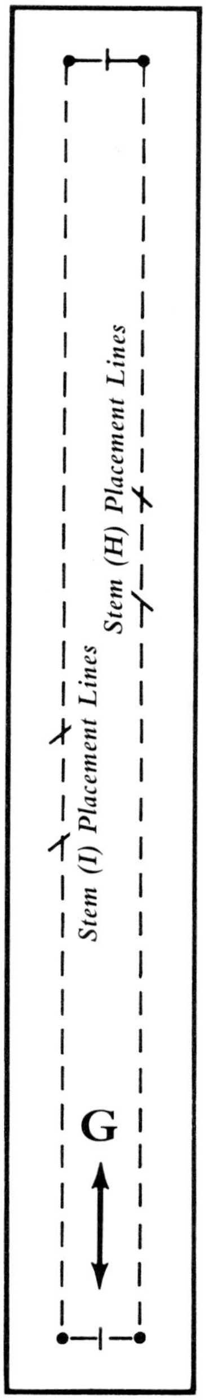
Stem (I) Placement Lines
Stem (H) Placement Lines
G

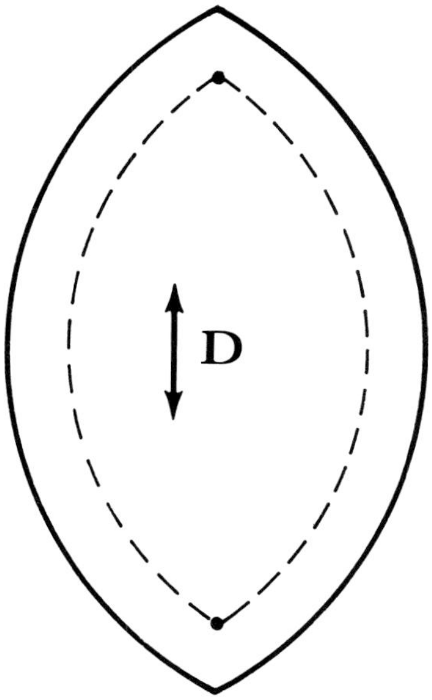
D

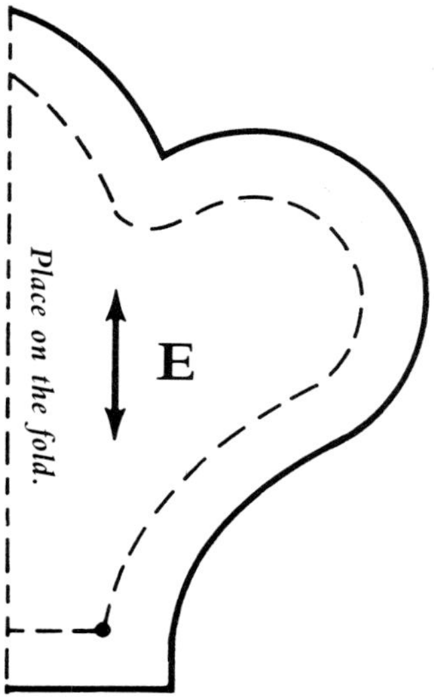
Place on the fold.
E

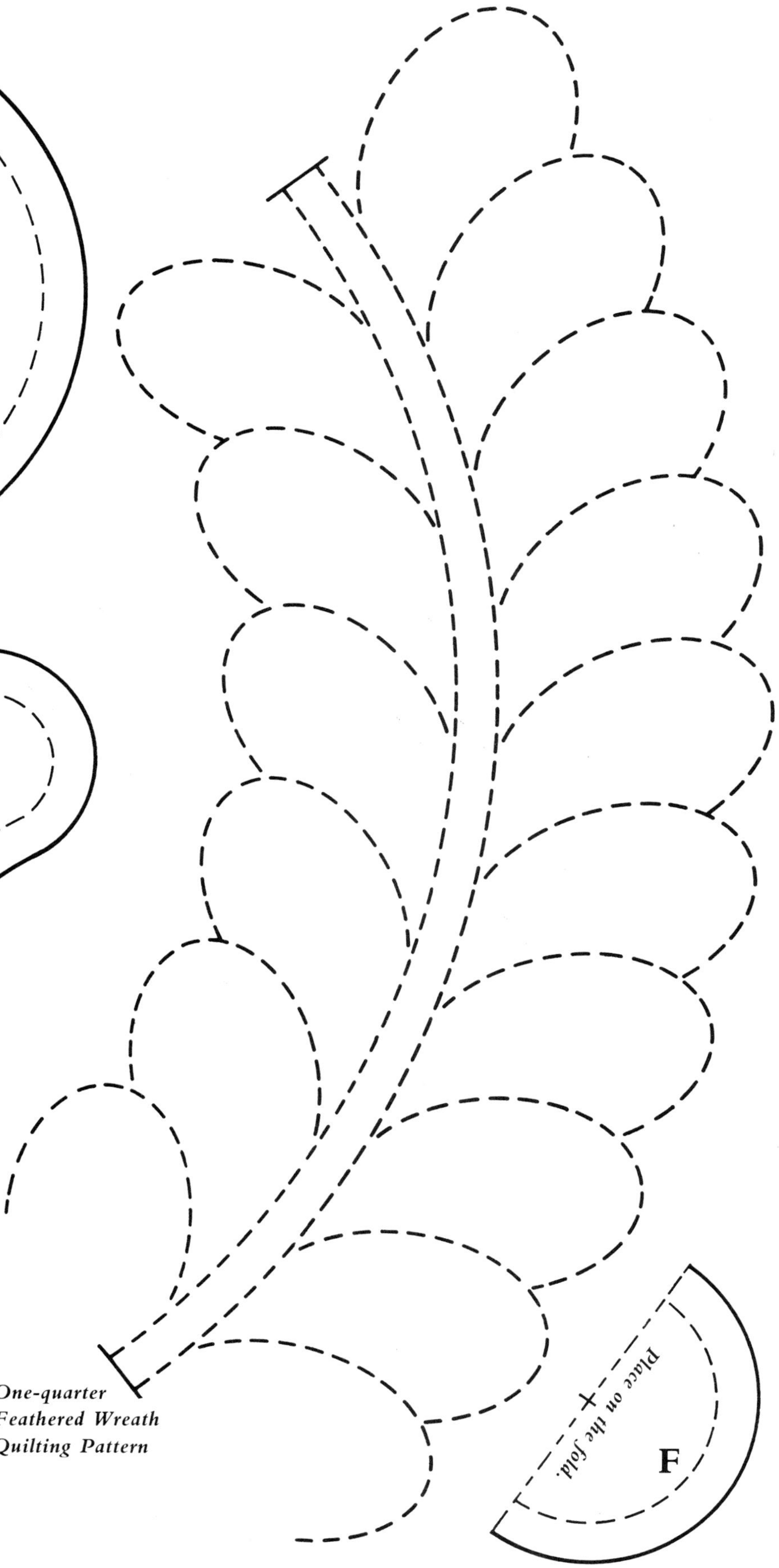
Place on the fold.
F

One-quarter Feathered Wreath Quilting Pattern

Quilting
Outline-quilt outside seam lines of all appliquéd pieces. Referring to quilt photograph, quilt a feathered wreath in the center of 4 of the appliquéd squares and join leaves with an arc of quilting. Quilt feathered waves along unappliquéd section of border strip.

Finished Edges
Bind with a continuous bias strip of red fabric.

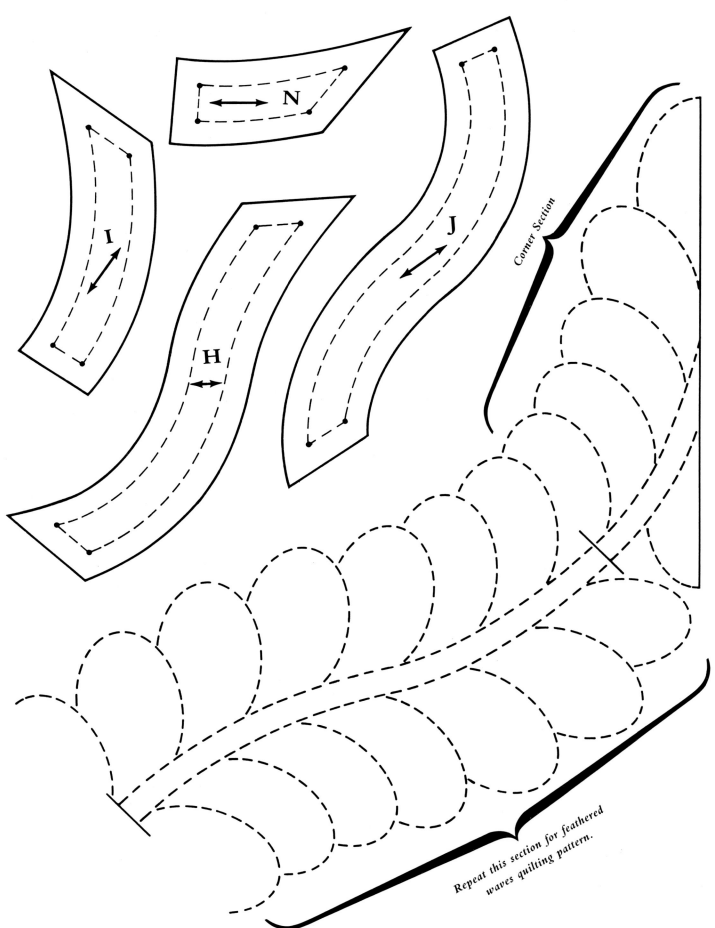

N

I

H

J

Corner Section

*Repeat this section for feathered
waves quilting pattern.*

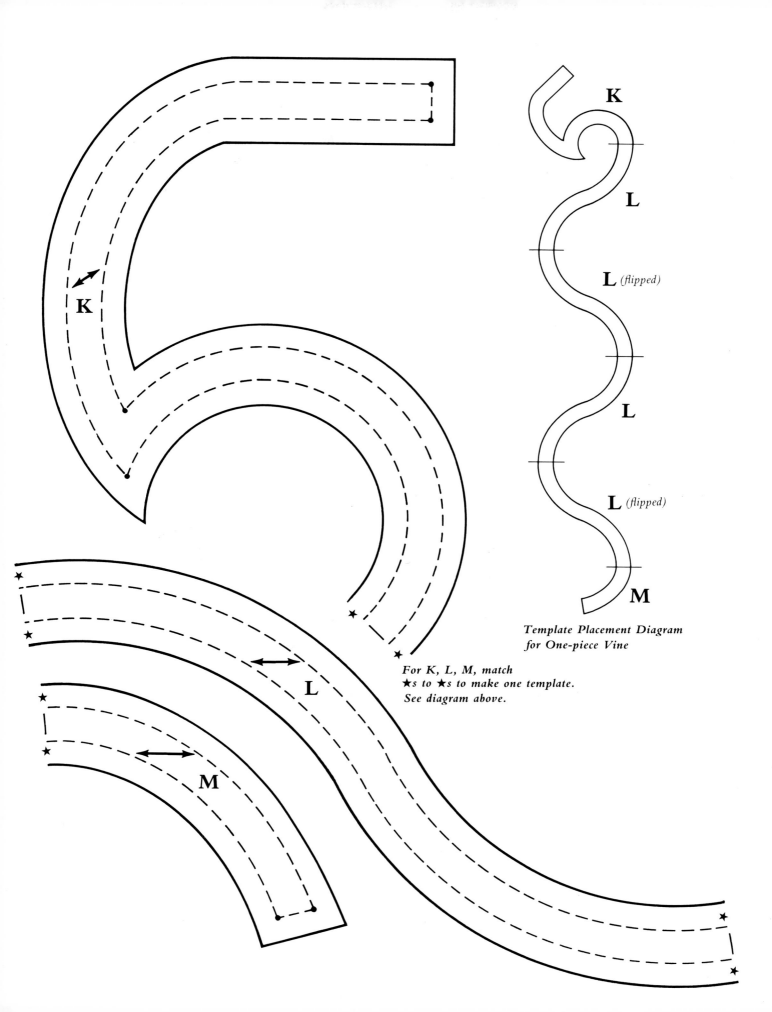

K

K

L

L *(flipped)*

L

L *(flipped)*

M

Template Placement Diagram
for One-piece Vine

L

For K, L, M, match
★s to ★s to make one template.
See diagram above.

M

Arthur A. Bluj

Winston-Salem, North Carolina

Storm at Sea
1986

A sailor's delight—a nautical treat is Arthur's stunning *Storm at Sea*. Arthur calmed the tempestuous sea with azure shades of blue and cast them upon an ocean floor of snow-white sand.

While sitting under a shade tree listening to tapes of Beethoven and Tchaikovsky, Arthur hand-pieced and hand-quilted *Storm at Sea* in five months. It was his second quilt to complete in one year, and as he says, "made for a wonderful time."

What about grandfathers? What do they do after they retire? For 35 years on the job as a telephone equipment repairman, Arthur heard multitudes of stories from ladies about their quilting grandmothers. The grandmothers filled their later years quilting, reaping hours of pleasure and satisfaction. Repeatedly, Arthur was told how grandfathers spent their days sitting around and longing for the good ole days. It just wasn't what Arthur had in mind for his retirement.

Influenced by these stories and a lot of determination not to be a rocking-chair grandfather, Arthur embarked on what he calls the biggest challenge of all—to learn to quilt. "After 99 hours of classes, a novice monster was turned loose on an unsuspecting quilting world," says Arthur. "My wife thinks I'm a little crazy, but she goes along with it."

Arthur belongs to four guilds in the Winston-Salem area—"mostly for learning new things," says Arthur. And claims, "All the quilters I've met are wonderful, easygoing, and helpful." Between quilting activities, Arthur has taken courses in upholstery, sewing, interior decorating, and modified tailoring. But he proudly states, "Quilting is for me. Life is much fuller, better, and happier since quilting."

Storm at Sea

Finished Quilt Size
76" x 88"

Number of Blocks and Finished Size
42 large blocks—8" x 8"
56 small blocks—4" x 4"
97 rectangular blocks—4" x 8"

Fabric Requirements
Dk. blue   —2½ yd.
Med. blue   —2¾ yd.
White   —3 yd.
Med. blue for
  bias binding   —1¼ yd.
Backing   —5 yd.

Number to Cut
Template A   — 42 med. blue
Template B   — 168 white
Template C   — 168 med. blue
Template D   — 97 dk. blue
Template E   — 388 white

Template F   — 56 med. blue
Template G   — 224 white
Template H   — 224 dk. blue

Quilt Top Assembly
1. Join square (A) and triangles (B and C), as shown in Block Piecing Diagram. Make 42 large blocks.

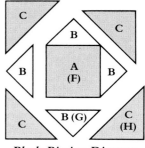

Block Piecing Diagram

2. Join square (F) and triangles (G and H) the same way, as shown in Block Piecing Diagram for Step 1. Make 56 small blocks.

3. Join a triangle (E) to each side of diamond (D) to form a rectangle. Make 97 rectangular blocks.

4. Refer to quilt photograph and alternate 7 small blocks with 6 rectangular blocks. Join *end-to-end,* beginning with a small block. Make 8 strips.

5. Refer to quilt photograph and alternate 7 rectangular blocks with 6 large blocks. Join at sides, beginning with a rectangular block. Make 7 rows.

6. Alternate strips with rows, beginning with a strip, and join lengthwise.

Quilting
Outline-quilt outside seam line of all blue pieces.

Finished Edges
Bind with a continuous bias strip of medium blue fabric.

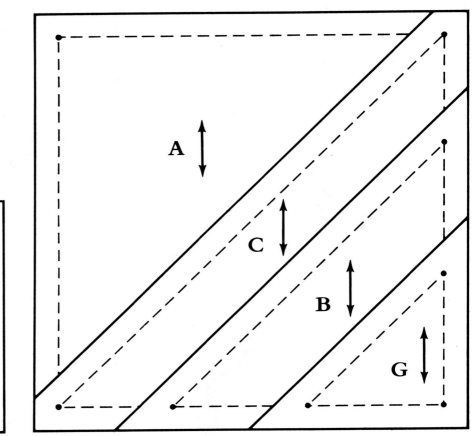

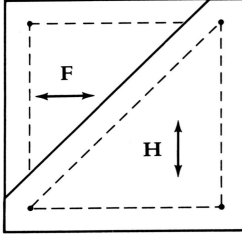

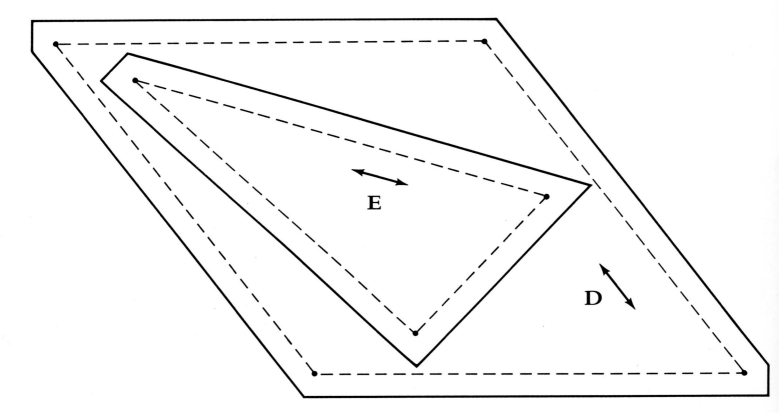

Rosemary Scott

Tonkawa, Oklahoma

One couldn't ask for a better quiltmaking teacher than an Amish grandmother. When Rosemary was a child, her Amish grandmother, Cora Mae Harshman, taught her to piece a friendship quilt. The desire to piece and design quilts has remained with her ever since. She is also an avid cattle rancher. Says Rosemary, "When I'm not taking care of my cattle or my family, I'm busy quilting."

Though her ranching duties may take her away from quilting, Rosemary usually has a quilt in progress. It's her way of ensuring that her children and grandchildren are never without a quilt. With four children and 14 grandchildren, that means a lot of quiltmaking. "And everyone has a quilt," says Rosemary. "Piecing quilts and giving them away are my greatest joys."

Lancaster Rose/Dresden Plate
1985

A luscious shade of strawberry ice cream pink is the background for a tick-tack-toe display of two recognizable traditional patterns. While the Lancaster Rose adopts the character of the X, the Dresden Plate supplies a fluffy, but essential, O. "I love to play with patterns," says Rosemary. "And the Lancaster Rose and Dresden Plate are two of my favorites." By including a pillow tuck, Rosemary always ensures that her patterns fall evenly on the bed.

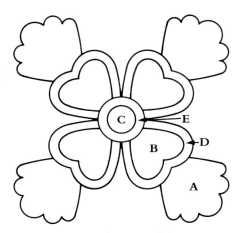

Lancaster Rose/Dresden Plate

Finished Quilt Size
Approximately 94″ x 116″

Number of Blocks and Finished Size
15 Lancaster Rose Blocks—
   15″ x 15″
15 Dresden Plate Blocks—
   15″ x 15″

Fabric Requirements
Pink   —8 yd.
Pink/white print I —3 yd.
Pink/white print II —1¼ yd.
Rose print I   —2 yd.
Rose print II   —½ yd.
Pink/white prints —2½ yd. total
Solid rose   —¼ yd.
Pink/white print II
  for bias binding —1¼ yd.
Backing   —8 yd.

Number to Cut
Template A —60 rose print I
Template B —60 rose print I
Template C —15 rose print I
Template D —60 pink/white
       print II
Template E —15 pink/white
       print II
Template F —225 assorted
       pink/white prints
Template G —15 solid rose
Template H —212 pink

Quilt Top Assembly
1. Cut thirty 15½″ squares from pink. Finger-crease each square on the diagonal; then finger-crease again on the opposite diagonal to find center and to form guidelines for appliqué.
2. For the Lancaster Rose pattern, lay out pieces (A-E), using the creases as guidelines. (See Lancaster Rose Placement Diagram.) Appliqué 15 squares.

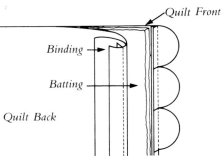

Lancaster Rose Placement Diagram

3. For the Dresden Plate pattern, join 15 plate pieces (F) at sides to form a circle. Center, baste, and appliqué to square. Finish block by appliquéing a circle (G) in the center of the plate pieces. Appliqué 15 squares.
4. Cut 76 sashing strips, 3″ x 15½″, from pink/white print I. Alternate 6 sashing strips with 3 Lancaster Rose blocks and 2 Dresden Plate blocks. Join strips and blocks at sides to form a row, beginning with a strip and a Lancaster Rose block. Refer to quilt drawing for proper block placement. Make 3 rows.
5. Alternate 6 sashing strips with 3 Dresden Plate blocks and 2 Lancaster Rose blocks. Join strips and blocks at sides to form a row, beginning with a strip and a Dresden Plate block. Refer to quilt drawing for proper block placement. Make 3 rows.
6. Cut forty-eight 3″ accent squares from rose print II. Alternate 6 accent squares with 5 sashing strips and join to form a strip row, beginning with an accent square. Make 8 rows.

7. Alternate strip rows with block rows. Begin with a strip row, then a Lancaster Rose row, 2 strip rows (for pillow tuck), a Dresden Plate row, a strip row, and continue alternating. Refer to quilt drawing for proper row placement. Join rows.
8. Cut one border strip, 4½″-wide, from pink and join to top of quilt.

Quilting
Outline-quilt outside seam lines of all appliquéd pieces. Quilt a small rose in the corners of each Dresden Plate block and between the rose petals of the Lancaster Rose block. Rosemary quilted a rope pattern along sashing strips and an *X*, reaching from corner to corner, in each accent square.

Finished Edges
With right sides together, stitch 2 half circles (H) together along curved edge. Clip seam, turn half circle right side out to form scallop, and press. With right sides and raw edges together, stitch 38 scallops side by side to each side through quilt *front* only. (See Scalloped Edge Diagram.) In the same manner,

Scalloped Edge Diagram

stitch 30 scallops to the bottom edge.

    Make a continuous bias strip, 1½″ wide, from pink/white print II. Referring to Scalloped Edge Diagram, pin binding strip edge ¾″ from sides and bottom edges of backing. With ¼″ seam allowance, stitch binding to quilt *back* only. Turn binding strip to cover backing and fold seam allowance under to meet seam line of scallops. Blind-stitch binding strip to scallops.

    Bind top edge with pink/white print II.

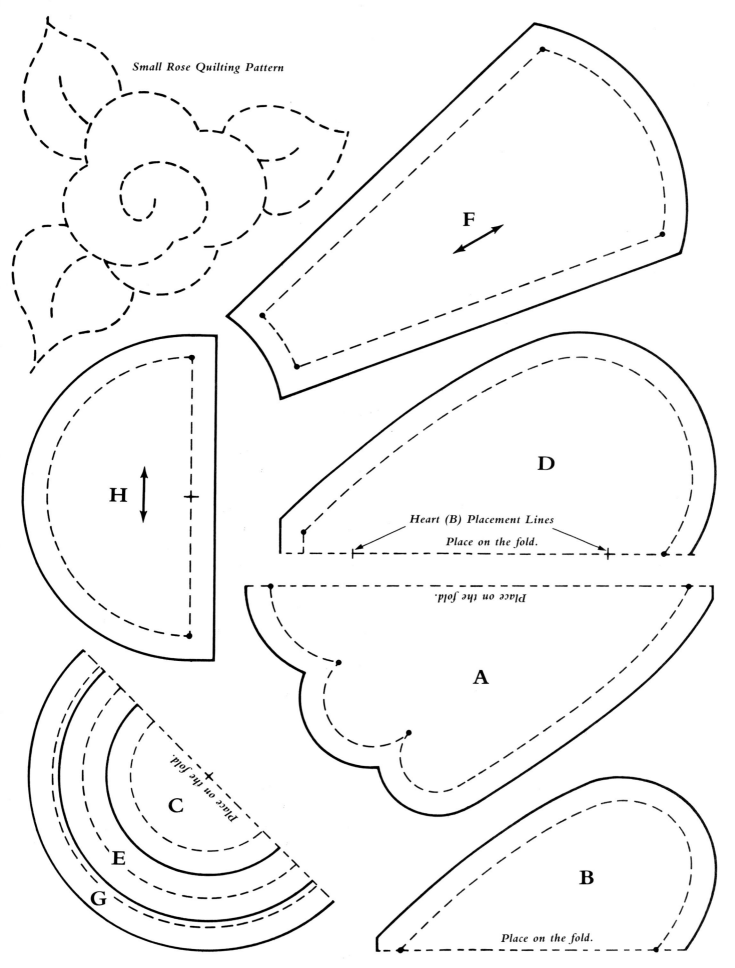

Small Rose Quilting Pattern

F

H

D

Heart (B) Placement Lines
Place on the fold.

Place on the fold.

A

C

Place on the fold.

E

G

B

Place on the fold.

Kit Carson
1984

When it comes to re-creating an old quilt, Laverne will stop at nothing. "When I spied a faded, worn-out quilt among much memorabilia at the Kit Carson Museum, I realized I had never seen one like it before," says Laverne. Before leaving the museum, she whipped up a few sketches, took a snapshot or two, and was on her way to duplicating her newest find. The original quilt was made in shades of blue with white triangles by Kit Carson's mother, Rebecca Robinson Carson. When Laverne finished her quilt, she took it to the museum, and the museum people were kind enough to take the original out of its case for her to see.

This *Kit Carson* won a red ribbon at the Baton Rouge National Quilting Association Show in 1984 and a blue ribbon at the Golden Triangle Quilt Guild Show in Beaumont, Texas, in 1985.

Laverne Noble Mathews

Orange, Texas

Quilters everywhere can appreciate the dedication of this enthusiastic quilt lover. Laverne confesses that her fondness for old quilts runs so deep that on occasion she has summoned genuine tears to get museum personnel to let her look at their collections. "Somewhere along the way it was borne in on me that the old quilts were the most fascinating," says Laverne. She has accumulated over 1,800 photographs of old quilts, and as an active member of the Texas Heritage Quilt Society, she has plenty of opportunities to view antique quilts of all kinds.

Now retired from public school teaching after 25 years, Laverne still maintains most of the creative activities she participated in as a teacher. Batik printing, book binding, rug hooking, and dressmaking are just a few of her side interests. But as Laverne describes it, "Quilting is the thing I have to do—a lovely compulsion. I have to have my quilting 'fix' daily."

Kit Carson

Finished Quilt Size
62" x 87"

Number of Feathered Triangles—36

Fabric Requirements
Beige	—4 yd.
Red	—2½ yd.
Red print	—1 yd.
Red for bias binding	—1¼ yd.
Backing	—5 yd.

Other Materials
Craft yarn, high loft	—4 oz. white
Tapestry needle	

Number to Cut
Template A	—36 beige
Template B	—248 beige
	320 red
Template C	—36 beige
Template D	—8 beige
Template E	—36 red print
Template F	—8 red print

Quilt Top Assembly
1. Join 4 red triangles (B) with 3 beige triangles (B) to form a strip, as shown in Feathered Triangle Piecing Diagram. Make 2 strips. Join one strip to the side of red print triangle (E) as shown. Join a beige square (A) to the end of the remaining strip and join to side of red print triangle (E) to complete feathered triangle. Make 36 feathered triangles.

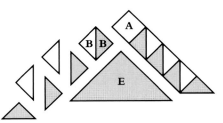

Feathered Triangle Piecing Diagram

To save time, string-piece all beige triangles (B) to red triangles (B) and use pieced squares as needed.

2. Join 4 red triangles (B) with 4 beige triangles (B), as shown in Half-Feathered Triangle Piecing Diagram. Join strip to side of red print triangle (F). Make 8 half-feathered triangles, as shown in Setting Diagram.

Half-Feathered Triangle Piecing Diagram

Setting Diagram

3. Refer to Setting Diagram and join feathered triangles (whole and half) with beige triangles (C and D) to form vertical strips. Make 8 strips and join lengthwise.

4. Cut 2 border strips, 5½″ wide, from beige and join to sides of quilt. Cut 2 more border strips, 5½″ wide, from beige and join to top and bottom of quilt.

5. Cut 4 border strips, 2¾″ wide, from red. Match straight edge of sawtooth guide with border strip edge. Mark sawtooth pattern on strip and trim. Lay sawtooth border strips on quilt, aligning quilt edge with straight edge of border. Appliqué triangle points to quilt and miter corners.

Quilting

Quilt feather pattern on beige triangles (C) of outside strips. Quilt parallel lines, ½″ apart, on the remaining areas of these triangles, beginning with a line ¼″ from seam line of triangle's side. Quilt pineapple motif on corner triangles (D).

Outline-quilt ⅛″ inside seam lines of all beige triangles (B) and

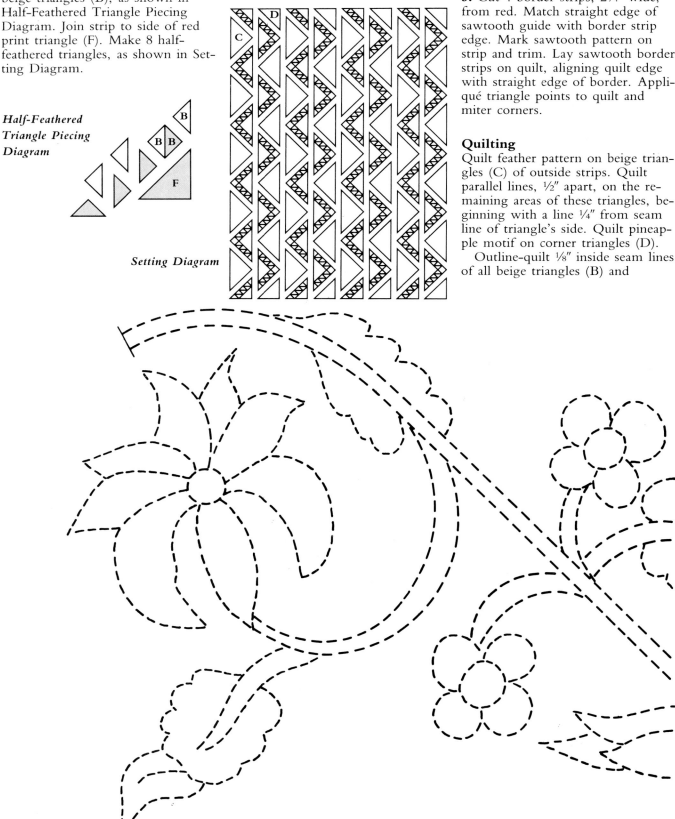

squares (A), only on sides adjacent to red triangles. Laverne followed the vertical printed pattern of her fabric in triangles (E and F) and quilted parallel lines 1″ apart.

Mark the vertical areas of beige fabric with Laverne's flowered vine and quilt. Quilt remainder of this area with parallel lines ⅜″ apart at a 45° angle.

Laverne used an unbroken rope pattern along beige borders and outline-quilted ⅛″ outside sawtooth seam line.

Trapunto for Flowered Vines
Thread a tapestry needle with doubled yarn and insert it into quilt at the beginning of flowered vine. (Trapunto can be done from front or back of quilt. Choose side where fabric most suitably closes itself over entry holes.) Push needle through the vine channel created by the quilting stitches on both sides. Bring needle out of the quilt when nearing the yarn's end. Holding yarn at other end, tug gently on threaded needle to straighten yarn in channel. Rethread needle and insert it in the hole just exited. Fill

flowers and leaves in same manner as vine. For wide areas, pull yarn through two or three times to fill the space.

Finished Edges
Bind with a continuous bias strip of red fabric.

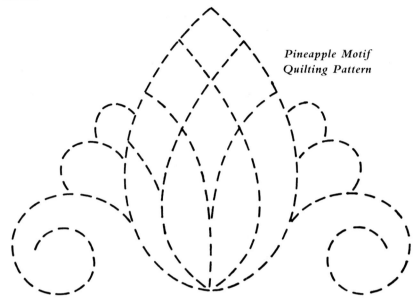

Pineapple Motif Quilting Pattern

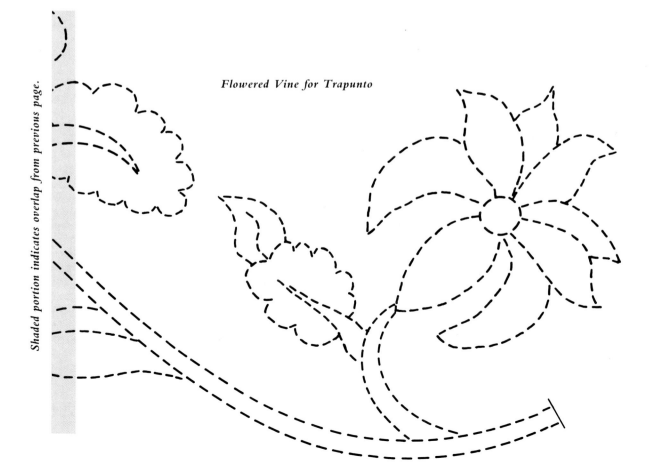

Flowered Vine for Trapunto

Shaded portion indicates overlap from previous page.

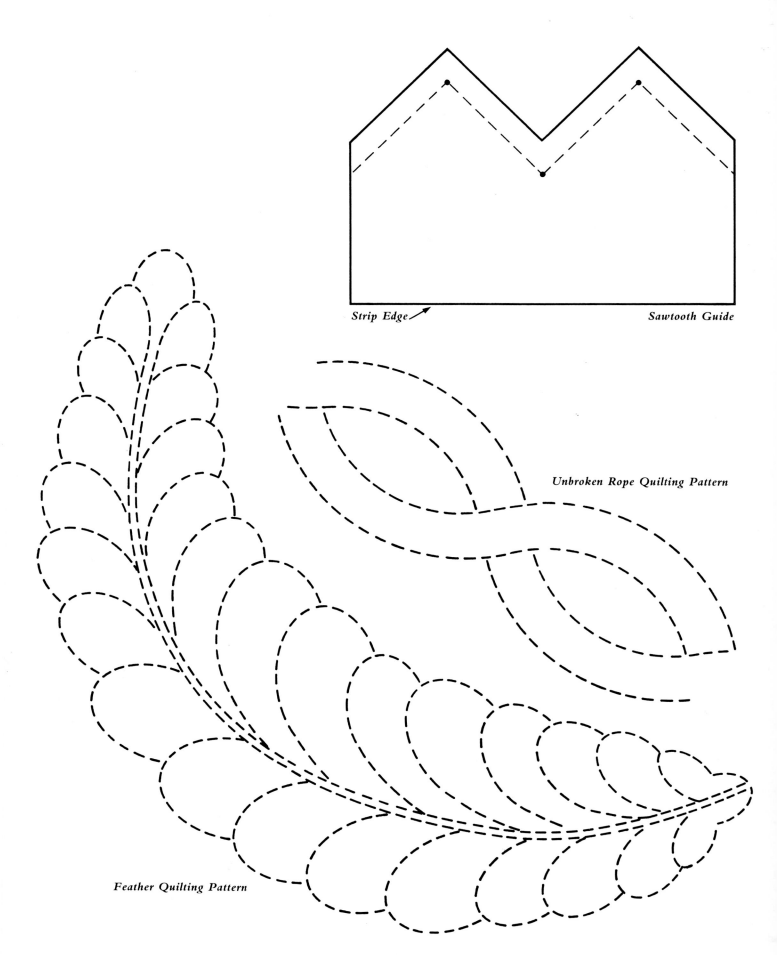

Strip Edge

Sawtooth Guide

Unbroken Rope Quilting Pattern

Feather Quilting Pattern

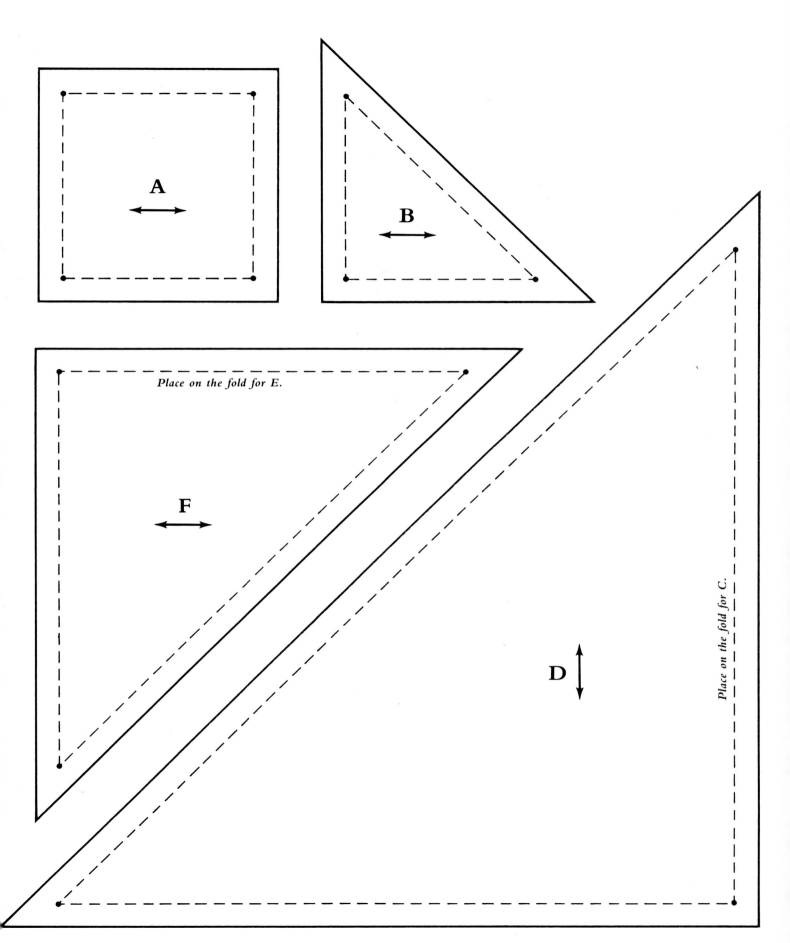

A

B

Place on the fold for E.

F

D

Place on the fold for C.

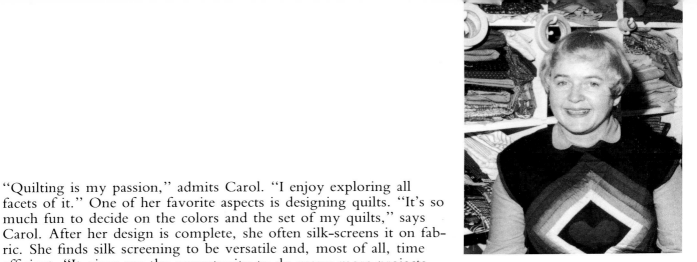

"Quilting is my passion," admits Carol. "I enjoy exploring all facets of it." One of her favorite aspects is designing quilts. "It's so much fun to decide on the colors and the set of my quilts," says Carol. After her design is complete, she often silk-screens it on fabric. She finds silk screening to be versatile and, most of all, time efficient. "It gives me the opportunity to do many more projects than I could do using only traditional methods," Carol says.

Carol started quiltmaking over 15 years ago and has continued to take quilting classes from as many different instructors as she can. "I draw my inspiration from my teachers and books," says Carol.

Carol Olson
Auberry, California

Checkered Hearts
1985

Here's a quilt to delight the checkerboard enthusiast. Carol's clever blend of contemporary color and design with the down-home charm of country hearts makes this quilt the perfect decor for a den, playroom, or game room. "I wanted to make my own brand of checkerboard, using hearts, my favorite design," says Carol.

To save time, Carol used black-and-white striped fabric to make her checkerboard. The checkerboard can also be made by cutting 3¾" squares and joining them in the checkerboard format. Hearts of turquoise, red, pink, pink-lavender, and the like are appliquéd to the checkerboard. Not only does *Checkered Hearts* look like fun, but as Carol assures us, "It was fun to make."

Checkered Hearts

Finished Quilt Size
58″ x 67″

Fabric Requirements
Black-and-white
  stripe★   — 1¼ yd.
(3¼″ stripes *across* the fabric)
Black-and-white
  stripe★   — 1¾ yd.
(⅝″ stripes *across* the fabric)
Royal blue   — 1¼ yd.
Blue   — 1½ yd.
Lavender   — 1½ yd.
Blue-green   — 1½ yd.
Green   — 1¾ yd.
Purple   — 1¾ yd.
Rose   — 1⅞ yd.
Heart colors   — ⅛ yd. each
Navy for
  bias binding   — 1 yd.
Navy for backing — 4 yd.
★ — If striped fabrics are not available, 1 yard each of white fabric and black fabric is required.

Number to Cut
Heart   —27 from shades
             of blue, green,
             red, and purple

Quilt Top Assembly
1. Cut 9 strips, 3¾″ wide, the length of the black-and-white fabric with 3¼″ stripes. (See Checkerboard Piecing Diagrams.) Stagger black-and-white strips lengthwise, as shown in Checkerboard Piecing Diagrams, and join. Continue joining strips until there are 9 squares across and 11 squares down. Trim any excess fabric around outside edges, leaving a ¼″ seam allowance.
2. Appliqué hearts inside squares in a random fashion or as shown.
3. Cut 4 strips, 2¾″ wide, from royal blue. Join to top and bottom first, and then to sides. Note: All strips for the remainder of quilt will be joined in this fashion unless otherwise noted.
4. Cut 4 strips, 2¾″ wide, from blue and join to quilt.
5. Cut 4 strips, 1¾″ wide, from lavender and join to quilt.
6. Cut 4 strips, 1½″ wide, from blue-green and join to quilt.
7. Cut 4 strips, 2¾″ wide, from green and join to quilt.
8. Make checkerboard border strips by cutting 8 strips, 1⅛″ wide, the length of the black-and-white fabric with ⅝″ stripes. Stagger and join strips in pairs in same manner as in Step 1. Join strips to quilt and trim any excess fabric, leaving a ¼″ seam allowance.
9. Cut 4 strips, 3″ wide, from purple and join to quilt.
10. Cut 4 strips, 2¼″ wide, from rose and join to quilt.

Quilting
Quilt in-the-ditch around checkerboard squares and outline-quilt along seam line of appliquéd hearts. (Carol used black quilting thread throughout.) Using your heart template for marking, quilt hearts in empty squares. Outline-quilt ¼″ inside seam lines of all border strips, except the checkerboard strips.

Finished Edges
Bind with a continuous bias strip of navy fabric.

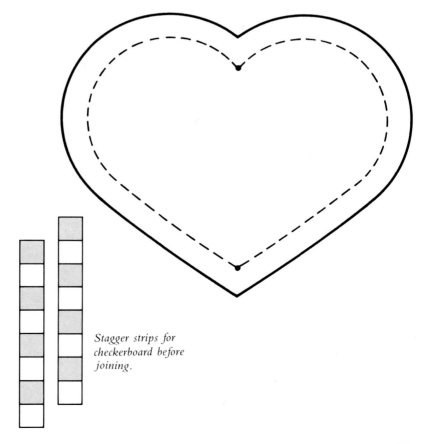

Checkerboard Piecing Diagrams

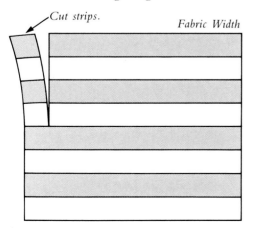

Cut strips.

Fabric Width

Stagger strips for checkerboard before joining.

Mountain Lake Isa
1985

The delicate ripples of a peaceful water lily pond are beautifully emulated with swirling lines of quilting on Rita's water lily wall hanging. While on a family vacation in Yellowstone National Park, Rita encountered a small water lily-filled lake. She knew then that she wanted to design a water lily quilt so the memory of that pond could be visualized forever in her home.

Greatly influenced by Joyce Schlotzhauer's technique for curved two-patch piecing (see "Resources"), Rita set about designing her Water Lily blocks. She confesses to the quilter, "My method requires complex piecing as well as more templates, but it means fewer pieces to cut and seams to sew in the finished piece."

To aid you with piecing, Rita suggests that you mark notches and sewing lines for ease in alignment.

Rita Erickson

Montclair, New Jersey

Rita believes that the reasons she began quilting are remarkably similar to those of many other quilters: being at home with small children, a need for outside interests, and a family heritage of quilts. Since 1971, quilting has filled her need for outside interests and introduced her to people and places that she never imagined. She enjoys teaching beginning and intermediate quiltmaking, though she sometimes finds that quilt-related activities cut into the time available to quilt.

Most of her recent quilts are either vaguely pictorial or are variations on the sampler quilt format. "My pictorial quilts are inspired by semi-abstract photographs, while my sampler quilts are 'one step beyond' familiar formats," says Rita. "I really enjoy the planning stage more than the construction stage." Along with originating the piecing designs, Rita says, "I do my own quilting, so that I can modify the design as I see the effect."

Mountain Lake Isa

Finished Quilt Size
56″ x 88″

Fabric Requirements

Dk. green (DG)	—	1¾ yd.
Lt. moss green (LMG)	—	¼ yd.
Med. moss green (MMG)	—	⅜ yd.
Dk. moss green (DMG)	—	½ yd.
Lt. peach 1 (LP1)	—	¼ yd.
Lt. peach 2 (LP2)	—	⅜ yd.
Med. peach 1 (MP1)	—	¼ yd.
Med. peach 2 (MP2)	—	⅝ yd.
Dk. peach (DP)	—	½ yd.
Lt. aqua (LA)	—	3½ yd.
Med. aqua (MA)	—	¼ yd.
Dk. aqua (DA)	—	½ yd.
Dk. aqua for bias binding	—	1 yd.
Backing	—	5 yd.

Number to Cut

Template A	—8 DG		Template F	—2 LP2
Template B	—8 DG			2 DP
	4 DMG		Template F★	—6 DMG
	8 MMG			2 MMG
	6 LP1			2 LMG
	4 MP2			2 LP2
	12 LA			2 DP
Template C	—14 DG		Template G	—4 DMG
	4 DMG			2 LP1
	8 MMG			4 LP2
	4 LMG			4 MP1
	16 DA			2 MP2
	12 MA			2 DP
	34 LA		Template G★	—2 DMG
	4 DP			2 LP1
Template D	—14 DG			6 LP2
	8 DA			4 MP1
Template E	—4 DG			2 DP
	2 DMG			2 MP2
Template F	—10 DMG		Template H	—2 LMG
(cont'd.)	4 MMG		(cont'd.)	6 DA

Template H   — 2 LA
                2 DMG
Template H★ — 6 DA
                6 LA
                2 DMG
Template I   — 16 LA
Template J   — 6 LA
Template J★ — 6 LA
Template K   — 2 MA
Template K★ — 2 MA
Template L   — 6 DG
                4 DMG
                2 LP2
                4 MP2
                2 DP
Template L★ — 6 DG
                2 DMG
                2 MMG
                4 MP2
                2 DP
Template M   — 2 MMG
Template M★ — 2 MMG
Template N   — 2 LP2
                4 MP2
                2 DP
Template N★ — 2 LP2
                4 MP2
                2 DP
Template O   — 4 DG
Template O★ — 4 DG
Template P   — 10 DG
Template Q   — 2 DG
Template Q★ — 2 DG
Template R   — 4 DG
Template S   — 2 LA
Template S★ — 2 LA
Template T   — 2 LA
Template T★ — 2 LA
Template U   — 2 DG
Template U★ — 2 DG
Template V   — 2 LA
Template V★ — 2 LA
Template W   — 2 DG
Template X   — 4 LA
Template X★ — 4 LA
Template Y   — 4 MP2
Template Y★ — 4 MP2

★ — Flip or turn over template if fabric is one-sided.

Number of Squares and Rectangles to Cut from Lt. Aqua★★

Square 1 — five 8½" x 8½"
Square 2 — four 6½" x 6½"
Rectangle 1 — two 10½" x 16½"
Rectangle 2 — four 4½" x 8½"
Rectangle 3 — four 6½" x 8½"
Rectangle 4 — four 6½" x 16½"
Rectangle 5 — eight 6½" x 10½"
Rectangle 6 — four 4½" x 6½"
Rectangle 7 — four 6½" x 12½"

★★ — Measurements include seam allowance.

Quilt Top Assembly

1. Refer to Setting Diagram, Block Piecing Diagrams for Blocks I through XII, and Color Code Charts. Begin with Row 1 and assemble blocks, as shown in Block Piecing Diagrams. Match marks on curves for accurate piecing. Clip curves, after joining pieces. Assemble blocks by rows, making the number of blocks indicated.

2. Join blocks in rows, as shown in Setting Diagram. Join rows.

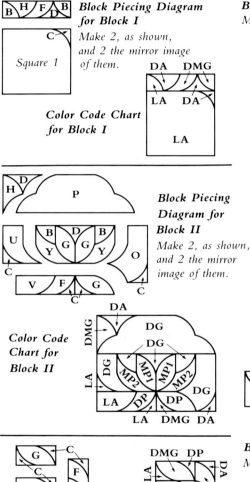

Block Piecing Diagram for Block I

Make 2, as shown, and 2 the mirror image of them.

Color Code Chart for Block I

Block Piecing Diagram for Block II

Make 2, as shown, and 2 the mirror image of them.

Color Code Chart for Block II

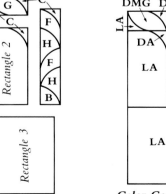

Block Piecing Diagram for Block III

Make 2, as shown, and 2 the mirror image of them.

Color Code Chart for Block III

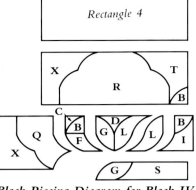

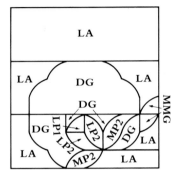

Block Piecing Diagram for Block IV
Make 2.

Color Code Chart for Block IV

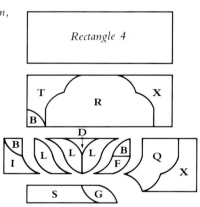

Block Piecing Diagram for Block V
Make 2.

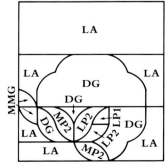

Color Code Chart for Block V

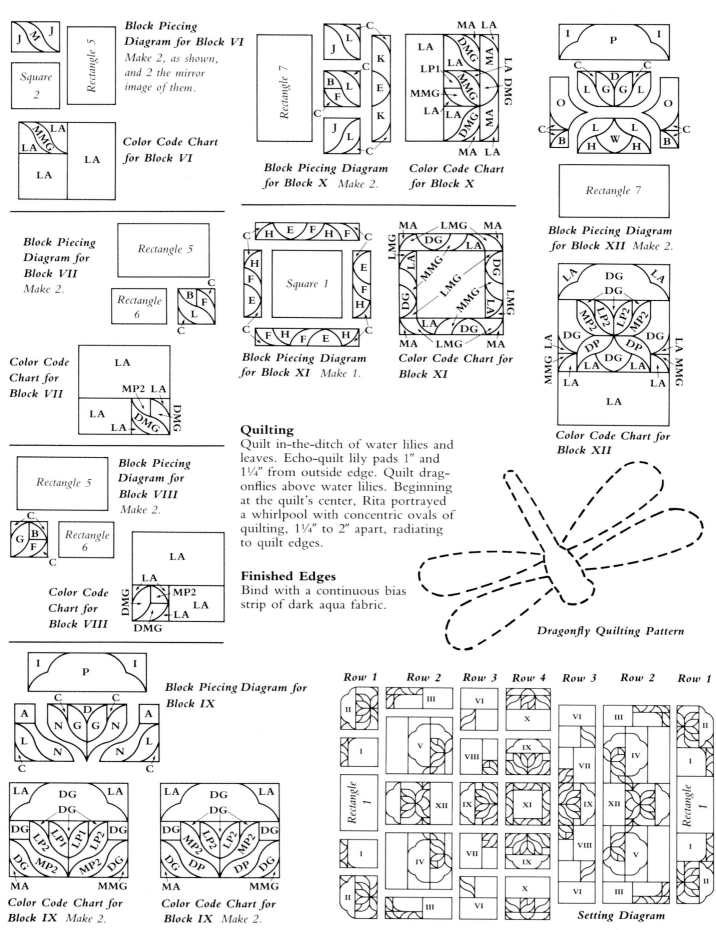

Block Piecing Diagram for Block VI *Make 2, as shown, and 2 the mirror image of them.*

Color Code Chart for Block VI

Block Piecing Diagram for Block VII *Make 2.*

Color Code Chart for Block VII

Block Piecing Diagram for Block VIII *Make 2.*

Color Code Chart for Block VIII

Block Piecing Diagram for Block IX

Color Code Chart for Block IX *Make 2.*

Color Code Chart for Block IX *Make 2.*

Block Piecing Diagram for Block X *Make 2.*

Color Code Chart for Block X

Block Piecing Diagram for Block XI *Make 1.*

Color Code Chart for Block XI

Block Piecing Diagram for Block XII *Make 2.*

Color Code Chart for Block XII

Quilting
Quilt in-the-ditch of water lilies and leaves. Echo-quilt lily pads 1″ and 1¼″ from outside edge. Quilt dragonflies above water lilies. Beginning at the quilt's center, Rita portrayed a whirlpool with concentric ovals of quilting, 1¼″ to 2″ apart, radiating to quilt edges.

Finished Edges
Bind with a continuous bias strip of dark aqua fabric.

Dragonfly Quilting Pattern

Setting Diagram

Row 1 Row 2 Row 3 Row 4 Row 3 Row 2 Row 1

79

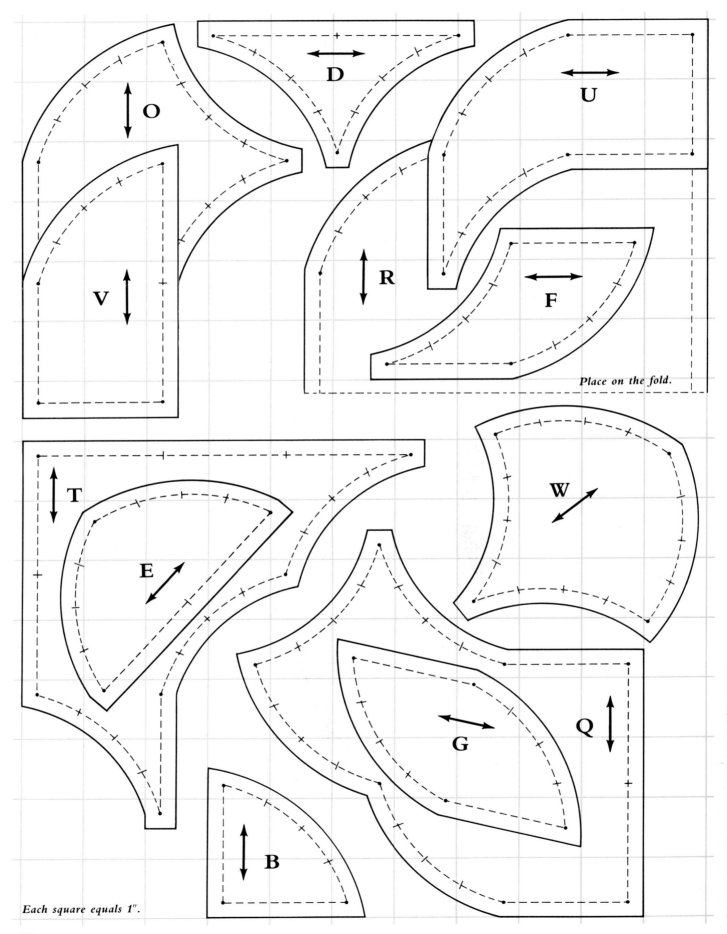

Place on the fold.

Each square equals 1".

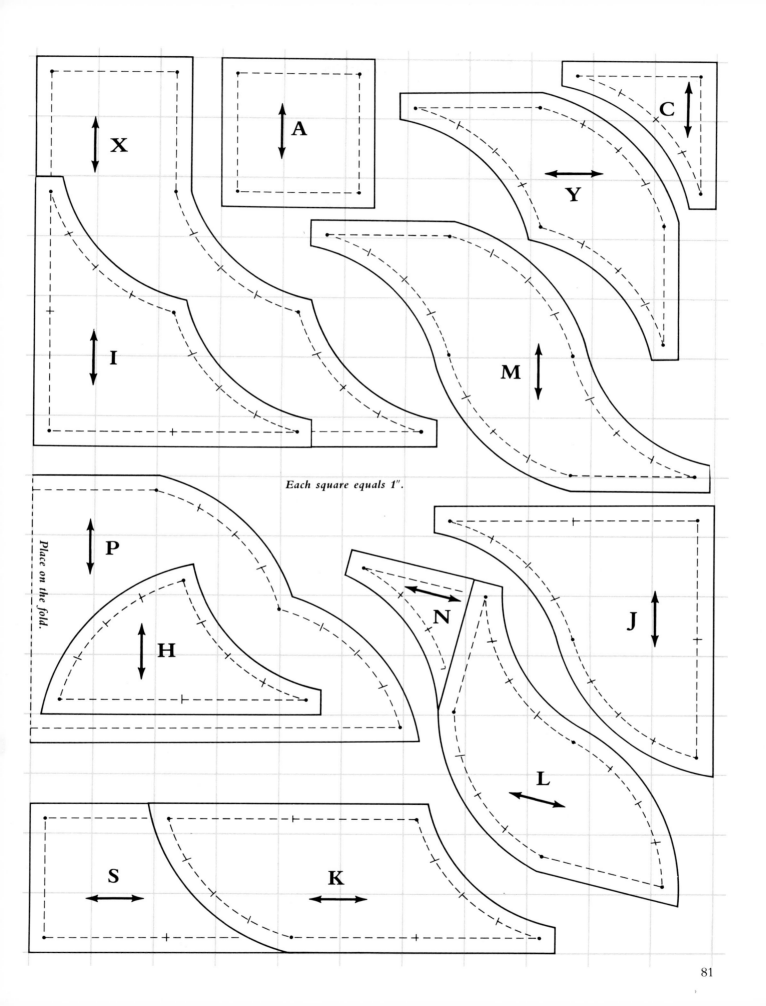

X

A

C

Y

I

M

P

Place on the fold.

H

Each square equals 1".

N

J

L

S

K

81

Norma Davis

Colorado Springs, Colorado

Norma likes to hand-piece quilts just about as much as she likes to travel. After she and her husband retired from their construction business some years ago, the roads out West beckoned them to taste adventure. And whether it's visiting one of their four children in California, North Dakota, New Mexico, or Kansas, or just traveling to a nearby lake on a fishing trip, those vast distances between towns provide plenty of "good piecing" times for Norma. There's no sewing machine in the trailer, but even if there were, Norma would choose to hand-piece. Says Norma, "I like it the best."

Her other craft interests range from crocheting to making stuffed animals as gifts for charity or a nearby nursing home. Presently, she is accessorizing each of her quilts by making a rag basket from the same fabrics as the quilt. Now, she boasts, "*Kissing Dinosaurs* has its very own rag basket."

Kissing Dinosaurs
1982

She saw dinosaurs instead of monkeys. Sounds like a title for a science fiction movie, but when Norma saw the Monkey Wrench block, she saw only dinosaurs. "My grandson, Aaron, was and still is crazy about dinosaurs," says Norma. "So, I added prairie points for the dinosaur's spikes, and there was my dinosaur."

History doesn't record whether dinosaurs ever kissed. Instead, we like to think this quilt symbolizes the love a grandmother can have for her grandson—enough to inspire her to attempt this as her first quilt.

Kissing Dinosaurs

Finished Quilt Size
72" x 92"

Number of Blocks and Finished Size
24 Dinosaur blocks—10" x 10"

Fabric Requirements
Yellow print	—1½ yd.
Green print I	—4 yd.
Green print II★	— ½ yd.
Muslin	—1½ yd.
Green print I for bias binding	—1¼ yd.
Backing	—5½ yd.

★ — For ease in folding dinosaur spikes, select a lightweight fabric.

Number to Cut
Template A	—48	yellow print
	48	muslin
Template B	—48	yellow print
	48	muslin
Template C	—48	yellow print
	48	muslin
Template D	—48	yellow print
	48	muslin

Quilt Top Assembly
1. Join 2 squares (A) of yellow print with 2 squares (A) of muslin to form a four-patch square. Join yellow print and muslin triangles (B) to sides of square, as shown in Block Piecing Diagram.

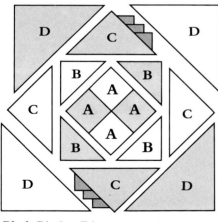

Block Piecing Diagram

2. Cut three 2" squares from green print II. Fold each square on the diagonal to form a triangle and fold triangle in half to make a dinosaur spike. Use marks on triangle (C) as guidelines and overlap 3 spikes on one side of a yellow print triangle. With right sides and raw edges together, stitch spikes in place with ¼" seam allowance. (See Spike Placement Diagram.) Make 2 yellow print triangles (C) with spikes for each block.

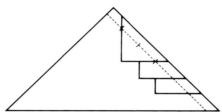

Spike Placement Diagram

3. Refer to Block Piecing Diagram and join yellow print and muslin triangles (C) and (D) to pieced square to complete block. Make 24 Dinosaur blocks.

4. Cut twenty-four 10½" squares from green print I. Refer to quilt drawing and alternate 3 solid squares with 3 Dinosaur blocks. Join squares to blocks at sides to form a row. Join rows.

5. Cut 2 border strips, 6½" wide, from green print I and join to top and bottom of quilt. Cut 2 border strips, 6½" wide, from green print I and join to sides of quilt.

Quilting
Outline-quilt ¼" inside dinosaur seam lines. Quilt across the diagonals of the green print squares.

Finished Edges
Bind with a continuous bias strip of green print I fabric.

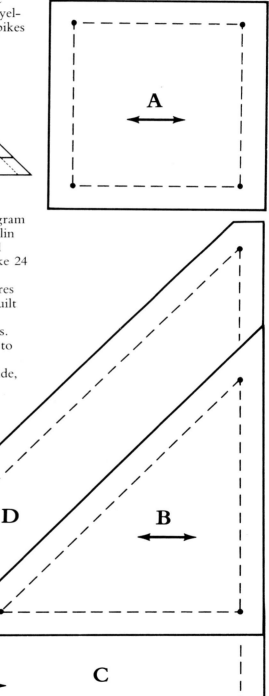

Tora Sterregaard

Phoenix, Arizona

Tora Sterregaard could be known as the quilting illusionist. She uses and adapts traditional quilt patterns in a way that makes it difficult to discover them. Her ingenious color selections and placements cause this deception. Tora calls these "color experiments." Routinely, before piecing these quilts, Tora shuffles, alters, and/or modifies paper copies of a chosen block in order to reach her design destination. Then the color experimenting begins. Tora colors each paper block with pencil until the color combinations satisfy her artistic goals.

A graduate of the Rhode Island School of Design, Tora began quilting while in college, by covering a blanket, and has been quilting ever since. Says Tora, "Quiltmaking provides the type of satisfaction that comes from creating a piece from start to finish, making all your own decisions."

Enjoy more of Tora's color experiments in our "Scraps to Spare" chapter.

Sedona Through the Trees
1984

South of Flagstaff, Arizona, in the Oak Creek Canyon of the Prescott National Forest, sits the town of Sedona. Dominated by an orange-red rocky terrain, Oak Creek Canyon's high-altitude environment can maintain only a minimum of broadleaf trees. *Sedona Through the Trees* is Tora's vision of the canyon as one would see it if peering through the trees to catch a glimpse of its brilliant orange landscape.

To make this stunning quilt, Tora enlisted the help of one of her favorite blocks, the Virginia Star. Its abundance of geometric shapes allowed Tora (as it will you) to capture with ease the undulation of color transitions from emerald greens to creamy oranges. Her love for this block and for Oak Creek Canyon is apparent in *Sedona Through the Trees.*

Sedona Through the Trees

Finished Quilt Size
84" x 84"

Number of Blocks and Finished Size
25 Star blocks—12" x 12"

Fabric Requirements
4 dark green (DG) prints
  DG1 — 2¼ yd.
  DG2 — 1 yd.
  DG3 — ¾ yd.
  DG4 — ⅓ yd.
3 medium greens (MG) (muted shades)
  MG1 (solid) — 2¼ yd.
  MG2 — ¾ yd.
  MG3 — ½ yd.
Light green print (LG) — ¼ yd.
2 light orange (LO) prints
  LO1 — ⅔ yd.
  LO2 — ¾ yd.
3 rust (R) prints
  R1 — ⅓ yd.
  R2 — ¼ yd.
  R3 — ⅓ yd.
DG1 for bias
  binding — 1 yd.
Backing — 7¼ yd.

Number to Cut
Template A	—	4 DG3
		4 MG2
		17 LO1
Template B	—	4 MG1
		80 MG3
		16 R2
Template C	—	8 DG1
		192 R1
Template D	—	32 DG2
		128 DG3
		128 MG1
		32 MG3
		72 LO2
		8 R2

Template E — 64 DG2
16 DG3
20 R3
Template E★ — 64 DG2
16 DG3
20 R3
Template F — 8 MG1
128 MG2
32 LG
32 LO1
Template G — 64 DG1
16 DG4
16 MG1
4 MG2
Template H — 16 DG1
12 MG1
Template I — 4 DG1
4 MG1
Template J — 4 LO2
Template K — 4 LG
Template K★ — 4 LG
Template L — 4 DG4
Template L★ — 4 DG4
Template M — 4 MG1
Template M★ — 4 MG1
Template N — 4 LO1
Template N★ — 4 LO1
Template O — 4 LO2
Template O★ — 4 LO2
Template P — 4 LO1
Template P★ — 4 LO1
Template Q — 4 MG1
Template Q★ — 4 MG1
Template R — 4 DG2
4 DG4
4 R3
Template S — 4 DG3
4 R1
4 R2
Template T — 4 DG1

★ — Flip or turn over template if fabric is one-sided.

Quilt Top Assembly

1. Refer to Color Code Chart for Middle Star Block (MSB). Join

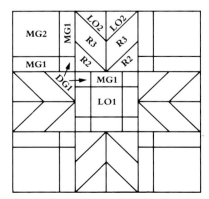

Color Code Chart for Middle Star Block

pieces into 9 small squares, join squares at sides to form 3 rows, and join rows to complete block. (See Star Block Piecing Diagram.) Make 1 Middle Star block.

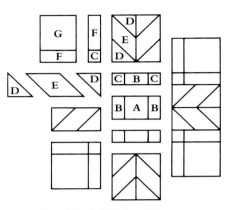

Star Block Piecing Diagram

2. Refer to Color Code Chart for Side Star Block (SSB). Join pieces in same manner as Star block in Step 1. Make 4 Side Star blocks.

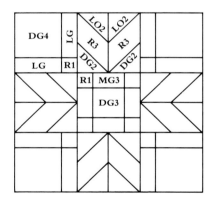

Color Code Chart for Side Star Block

3. Refer to Color Code Chart for Corner Star Block (CSB). Join pieces in same manner as Star block in Step 1. Make 4 Corner Star blocks.

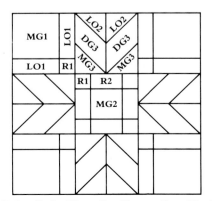

Color Code Chart for Corner Star Block

4. Join Star blocks at sides to make 3 rows of 3 blocks each, as shown in Setting Diagram for Center Unit. Join rows.

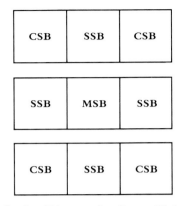

Setting Diagram for Center Unit

5. Refer to Color Code Chart for Corner Sections. Start with triangle (J) and sew flipped strip (K) to short leg of triangle, as shown in Medallion Assembly Diagram. Join square (S) to strip (K) and join to other side of triangle. Continue joining strips and squares to sides of pieced triangle. Make 4 corner sections. Join 1 corner section to each side of center unit.

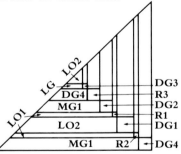

Color Code Chart for Corner Sections

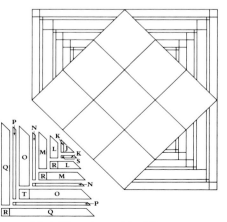

Medallion Assembly Diagram

6. Refer to Color Code Chart for Border Star Block (BSB). Join pieces in same manner as Star block in Step 1. Make 16 Border Star blocks.

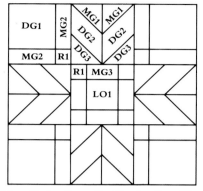

Color Code Chart for Border Star Block

7. Join 3 Border Star blocks with 2 medium green triangles (H), 2 medium green triangles (I), and 2 dark green triangles (H), as shown in Short Border Piecing Diagram. Make 2 short borders. Join border edge with medium green triangles to sides of quilt.

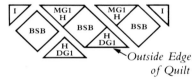

Short Border Piecing Diagram

8. Join 3 Border Star blocks with 4 medium green triangles (H) and 2 dark green triangles (H), as shown in Long Border Piecing Diagram. Make 2 long borders. Join border edges with medium green triangles to top and bottom of quilt.

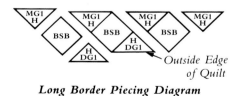

Long Border Piecing Diagram

9. Join dark green triangles (H and I) to sides of Border Star block, as shown in Corner Piecing Diagram. Make 4 and join to quilt.

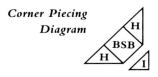

Corner Piecing Diagram

Quilting
Tora suggests outline-quilting all Star blocks by following the piecing. Quilt large areas of medium green, that is, triangles (H and I) and strips (Q), as shown in Quilting Diagram. Parallel lines within Celtic knot pattern are ½″ and 1″

apart, respectively. Horizontal parallel lines on dark green triangles are 1½″, 2½″, and 3″ from seam line.

Finished Edges
Bind with a continuous bias strip of DG1 fabric.

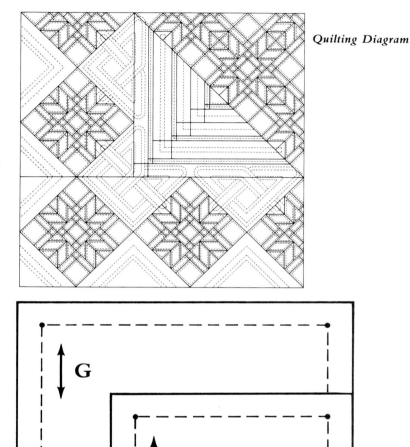

Quilting Diagram

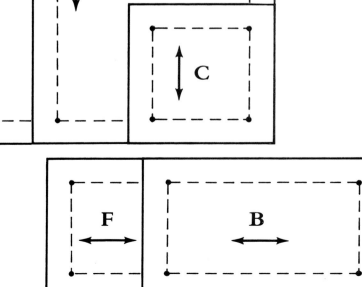

87

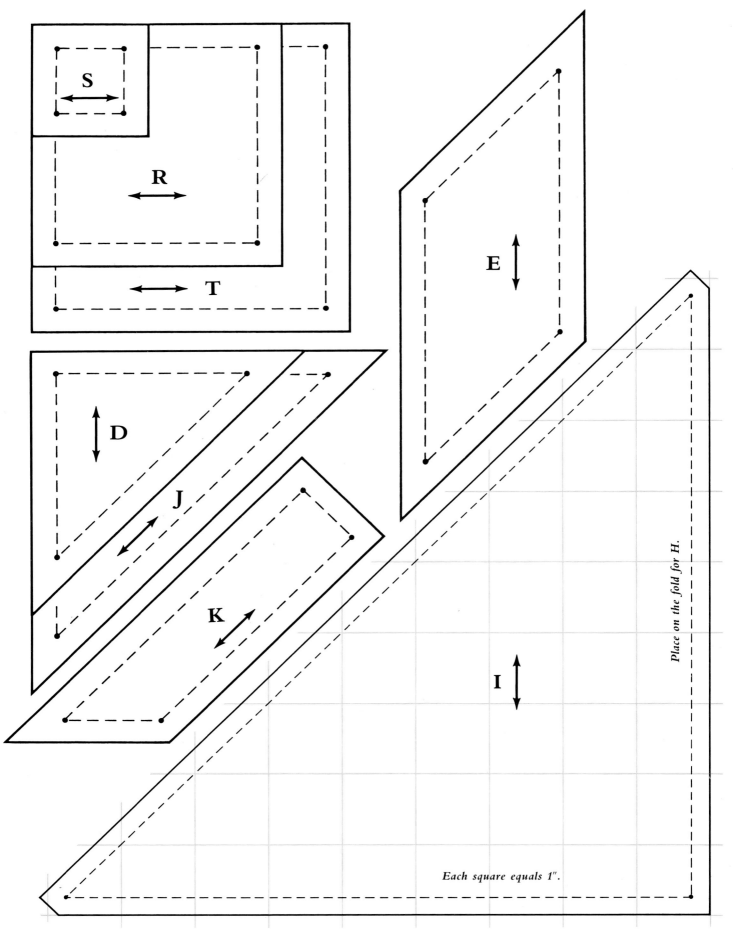

S

R

T

E

D

J

K

I

Place on the fold for H.

Each square equals 1".

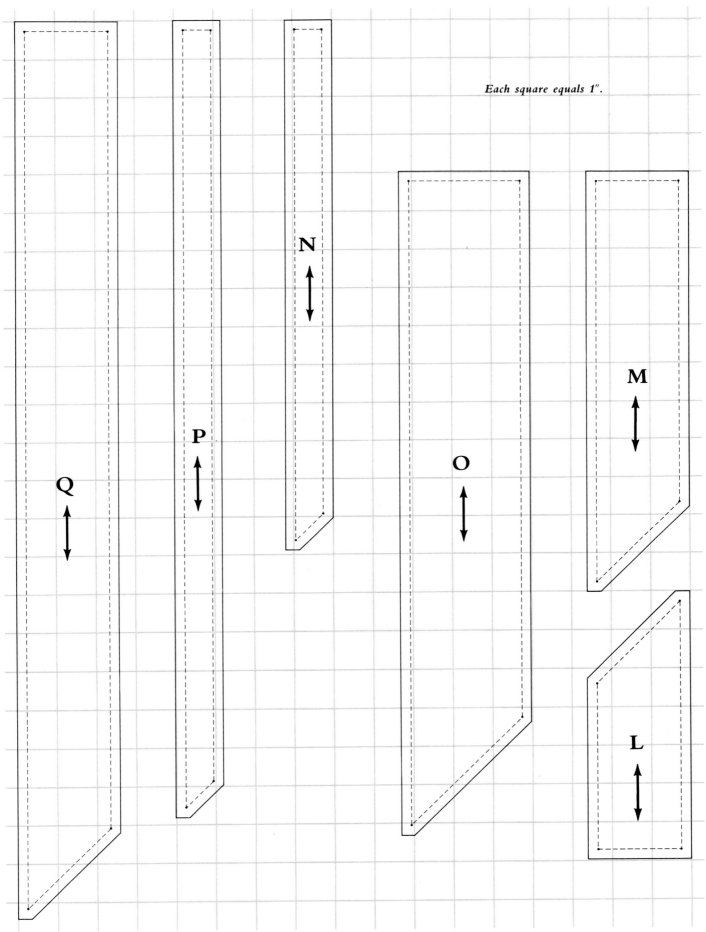

Each square equals 1".

Donna McCulloch

Klamath Falls, Oregon

My Daisy
1982

Large, bright daisies gracefully pose themselves amid strips of apple green to remind us of the warmth and sparkle of a summer's day. "*My Daisy* was one of my first tries at creating my own design and gave me the courage to try other things on my own," says Donna. While she was making a Double Wedding Ring quilt, some of the extra pieces dropped on the floor, and the interesting dispersion of the fabric pieces inspired her daisy pattern. So it is easy to see why Donna claimed these daisies as her own.

Machine-appliquéd, the daisies take very little time to anchor to their blocks. Once joined in rows, the splendor of these cheerful denizens of summer emits a radiance of energy and hope that invites a smile and an outdoor picnic.

Here's a mother who has discovered the cure for the empty nest syndrome—quilting. When three of her five children were raised and ready to leave the nest, Donna learned to quilt. "As each child left home I found that I had a little more time to donate to quilting," says Donna. "I've almost looked forward to their leaving, counting the extra time I would have to quilt!"

Donna quilts mainly for pleasure, but admits she gains a great deal of pleasure from the ones she's sold. The money comes in handy for quilting supplies and equipment, and the acknowledgement of her expertise encourages her to go on to bigger and better projects. "Quilting has made me feel creative, like an explorer in an old wilderness," says Donna.

My Daisy

Finished Quilt Size
91" x 107"

Number of Blocks and Finished Size
16 blocks—20" x 24"

Fabric Requirements
White   — 5½ yd.
Yellow   — 2½ yd.
Apple green (includes yardage
    for bias binding) — 4¼ yd.
Dk. brown   — ¼ yd.
Backing   — 8 yd.

Other Materials
Lightweight
    fusible interfacing — 5¾ yd.
Fabric-compatible glue stick
Freezer paper

Number to Cut
Template A   — 112 yellow
Template B   — 32 apple green
Template C   — 16 dk. brown

Quilt Top Assembly
1. Cut 16 background blocks, 21" x 24½", from white. Make a master pattern by laying pattern pieces on a piece of freezer paper the same size as the white block. (See Placement Diagram.) Draw around the

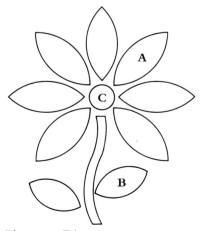

Placement Diagram

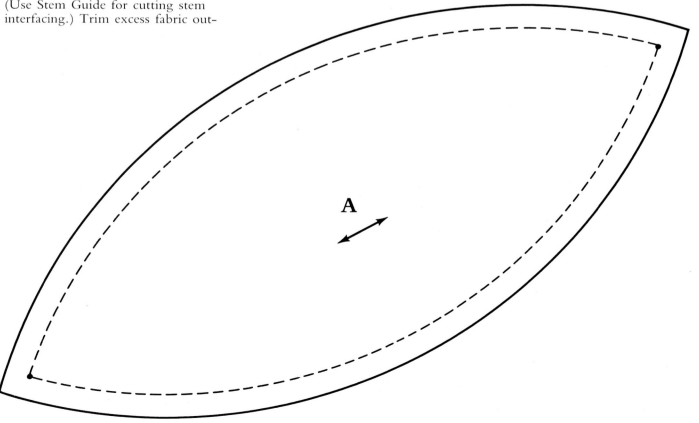

pieces with a wide felt-tip pen. Pin background blocks to freezer paper so that lines show through to help you position the daisy pieces.
2. For daisy stem, make a continuous bias strip, 1½″ wide, from apple green. Prepare daisy pieces (A, B, C, and stem) for machine-appliquéing by applying lightweight fusible interfacing to each piece. (Use Stem Guide for cutting stem interfacing.) Trim excess fabric out-

side seam line. Anchor pieces to block, using a glue stick. Satin-stitch over raw edges, using thread the same color as the piece. Appliqué 16 daisy blocks.
3. Cut 12 sashing strips, 2¾″ x 24½″, from apple green. Alternate 4 appliquéd blocks with 3 sashing strips and join at sides, beginning

with an appliquéd block to form a row. Make 4 rows.
4. Cut 12 sashing strips, 2¾″ x 21″, from apple green. Cut nine 2¾″ accent squares from yellow. Alternate 3 accent squares with 4 sashing strips and join, beginning with a sashing strip to form a row. Make 3 rows.
5. Alternate block rows with strip rows and join, beginning with a block row. Be sure all daisies are right side up.
6. Cut 4 border strips, 2¾″ wide, from apple green. Join to top and bottom and then to sides of quilt.

Quilting
Outline-quilt around all daisy pieces. Quilt parallel diagonal lines in background at a 45° angle and 1″ apart, alternating directions for blocks beside each other. Use your favorite quilting pattern for border strips.

Finished Edges
Bind with a continuous bias strip of apple green fabric.

A

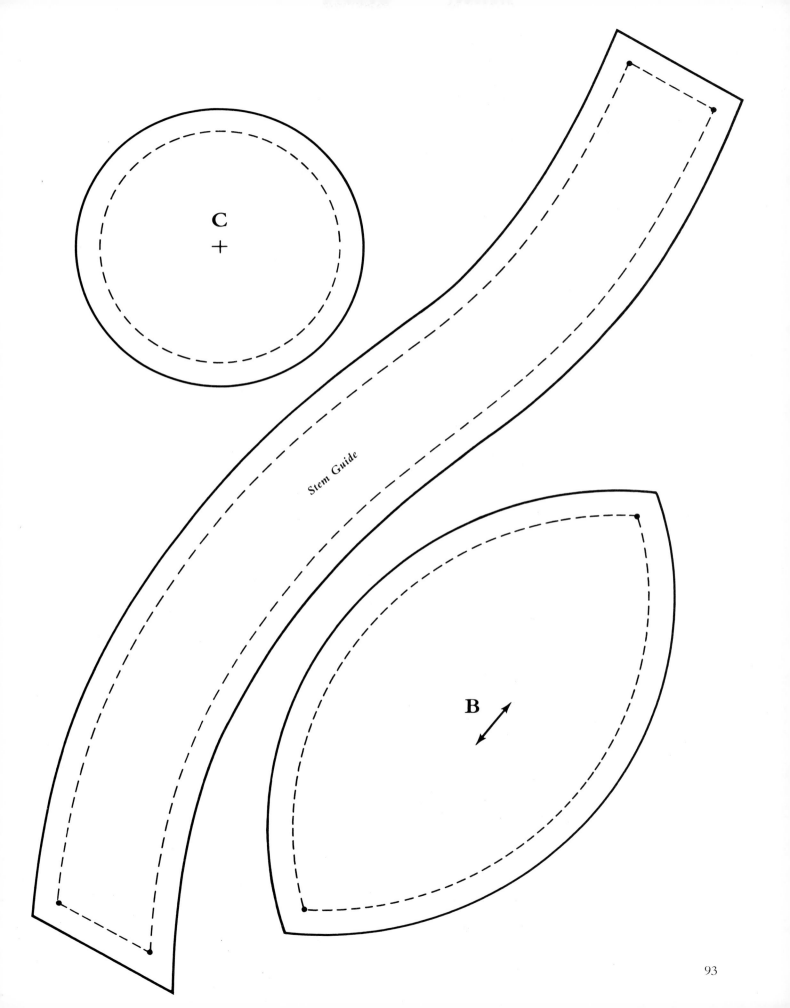

C
+

Stem Guide

B

Sylvia Whitesides

Lafayette, Indiana

"It all comes together," says Sylvia. "My love for sewing and needlework, my knowledge of color, my degree in interior design, and my work as a color consultant—it all comes together in quilting." At first Sylvia's family thought her quilting was just another phase she was going through, and all her quilting would end up in a pile of unfinished projects. "But," she says proudly, "I'm still going strong after almost three years."

Disappointed by the limited number of color gradations in fabrics available for purchase, Sylvia plunged into hand-dyeing her own fabrics. In this way she could achieve the color specifications she desired. "I mixed paints as a decorator and color consultant," says Sylvia. "So, why couldn't I mix dyes?" After an unsuccessful experience with domestic dyes, however, Sylvia became frustrated with the idea of hand-dyed fabrics. (See Sylvia's Notes on Hand-Dyeing Fabric.) "But I loved the beautiful shades of colors," says Sylvia. "Two years later, I decided to try again." This time, after she had researched the topic and discovered fiber-reactive dyes, her hand-dyed fabrics satisfied her needs in every way.

Now Sylvia experiments with overdyeing fabric prints. "I find it an interesting way to fix some ugly fabrics," says Sylvia. "I also recommend fabric painting as a fun and exciting way to produce your own designs." Visit with Sylvia a little more as she shares her hand-dyeing expertise with us in a special section following her quiltmaking instructions.

Facets
1987

Packed between the spokes of the color wheel are scores of color gradations just waiting to be put into service. Sylvia's *Facets* dazzles our eyes with the rich shades found between the secondary colors of violet and green. "For this quilt, any colors will do," says Sylvia, "but it is important to choose those which are side by side on the color wheel."

All fabrics are hand-dyed with Procion® M-series fiber-reactive dyes. Yardages of bleached and unbleached muslin are hand-dyed to produce bright and muted shades, respectively. Sylvia placed the brighter shades in the quilt's center and the muted shades in the outer areas. "I wanted the quilt to look as if there were a light source in the center," says Sylvia.

Fabric requirements and complete directions for hand-dyed fabrics are given below. If you are not too keen on the idea of hand-dyed fabrics, purchased-fabric requirements are also given with shade gradations indicated. Many large fabric stores and/or mail-order companies sell fabrics in shade gradations that would work very well with this type of quilt.

Facets

Finished Quilt Size
48" x 60"

**Fabric Requirements
for Hand Dyeing**
Bleached 100%
   cotton muslin   —6¼ yd.
Unbleached 100%
   cotton muslin★   —11½ yd.
★ — Includes 2 yards for backing and binding.

**Amount to Dye of
Each Shade★★**
From bleached muslin:
Teal, bright (TB)
   TB1 — ½ yd.
   TB2 — ½ yd.
   TB3 — ½ yd.
   TB4 — ½ yd.
   TB5 — ⅜ yd.
   TB6 — 1 yd.
   TB7 — 1 yd.
★★ — See footnote on next page.

Raspberry, bright (RB)
RB1 — 1 yd.
RB2 — ½ yd.
RB3 — ½ yd.
RB4 — ½ yd.
RB5 — ⅜ yd.
Purple, bright (PB)
PB4 — ½ yd.
PB5 — ½ yd.
PB6 — ½ yd.

From unbleached muslin:
Teal, muted (TM)
TM1 — ½ yd.
TM2 — ½ yd.
TM3 — ½ yd.
TM4 — ½ yd.
TM5 — ⅝ yd.
Raspberry, muted (RM)
RM2 — ½ yd.
RM3 — ½ yd.
RM4 — ½ yd.
RM5 — ⅝ yd.
RM6 — 2¾ yd.†
RM7 — 1 yd.
Purple, muted (PM)
PM3 — 1 yd.
PM4 — ½ yd.
PM5 — ½ yd.
PM6 — ½ yd.
PM7 — 1 yd.
** — Shades range from 1 through 7, with 1 being the lightest. Yardages for hand dyeing are greater

than for purchased fabrics, because these dye recipes work best with one yard of 44"-wide fabric. If you use less yardage, fabric will dye to a shade different from the required shade. Excess yardage is also given to allow for shrinkage and fraying of fabric.

See directions for hand-dyeing fabric at the end of these quiltmaking instructions.

† — Includes yardage for backing and binding.

Purchased Fabric Requirements***
Teal, bright (TB)
TB1 — ⅛ yd.
TB2 — ⅛ yd.
TB3 — ⅛ yd.
TB4 — ⅛ yd.
TB5 — ⅛ yd.
TB6 — ⅛ yd.
TB7 — ⅛ yd.
Raspberry, bright (RB)
RB1 — ⅛ yd.
RB2 — ⅛ yd.
RB3 — ⅛ yd.
RB4 — ⅛ yd.
RB5 — ⅛ yd.
Purple, bright (PB)
PB4 — ⅛ yd.
PB5 — ⅛ yd.
PB6 — ⅛ yd.

Teal, muted (TM)
TM1 — ⅛ yd.
TM2 — ½ yd.
TM3 — ½ yd.
TM4 — ½ yd.
TM5 — ⅝ yd.
Raspberry, muted (RM)
RM2 — ⅛ yd.
RM3 — ⅛ yd.
RM4 — ¼ yd.
RM5 — ⅝ yd.
RM6 — ⅝ yd.
RM7 — ½ yd.
Purple, muted (PM)
PM3 — ⅛ yd.
PM4 — ⅛ yd.
PM5 — ⅛ yd.
PM6 — ⅛ yd.
PM7 — ⅛ yd.
Raspberry, muted, for backing and binding — 2 yd.
*** — If you do *not* plan to hand-dye your fabrics, use this list. Purchase fabrics in shade gradations, with 1 being the lightest.

Number to Cut
Template A   —2 TB1
                4 TB2
                6 TB3
                8 TB4
                6 TB5
                4 TB6
(cont'd.)   2 TB7

Quilt Top Assembly
1. Refer to Color Code Chart and quilt photograph before piecing. Notice that the color pattern for one quarter repeats itself, either in reverse or as a mirror image.
2. Join 4 diamonds (A) to form one large diamond, as shown in Piecing and Setting Diagram. Make 48 large diamonds.
3. Join 1 diamond (A) with 2 triangles (C) to form a long half

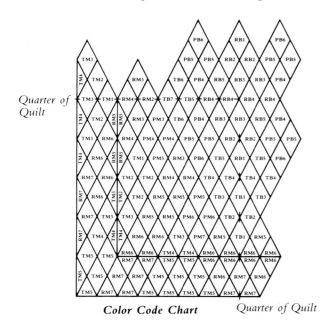

Color Code Chart   Quarter of Quilt

Quarter of Quilt

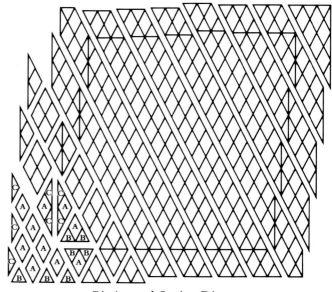

Piecing and Setting Diagram

Template A — 2 RB1
4 RB2
4 RB3
4 RB4
2 RB5
4 PB4
8 PB5
4 PB6
6 TM1
16 TM2
18 TM3
4 TM4
24 TM5
2 RM2
8 RM3
14 RM4
20 RM5
28 RM6
18 RM7
4 PM3
8 PM4
8 PM5
8 PM6
4 PM7
Template B — 8 TM4
24 TM5
24 RM6
20 RM7
Template C — 4 TM2
4 TM3
16 TM4
4 TM5
16 RM5
8 RM7

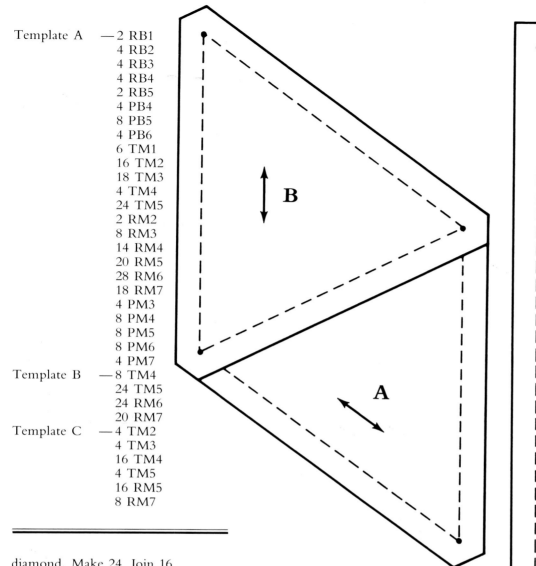

diamond. Make 24. Join 16 lengthwise, as shown in Piecing and Setting Diagram.

4. Join 1 diamond (A) with 2

Quilting Diagram

triangles (B) to form a short half diamond. Make 40. Join 12, as shown in Piecing and Setting Diagram.

5. Refer to the Color Code Chart, and Piecing and Setting Diagram. Arrange diamonds in diagonal rows and join at sides. Join rows.

6. Cut backing 1″ larger than quilt top on all four sides for a rolled-hem binding.

Quilting

Refer to Quilting Diagram and quilt parallel lines as shown. Parallel lines are ¾″ and 1½″ apart. Sylvia added curved quilting lines to give a gemstone effect to the center area.

Finished Edges

Roll backing to the front, turn under a ¼″ seam allowance, and blindstitch in place.

Sylvia's Notes on Hand-Dyeing Fabric

Through trial and error and a little research, I learned that fiber-reactive dyes, such as the Procion® M-Series, were not as sensitive to light and were more colorfast than the domestic dyes. Initially, I tried the washing-machine methods for dyeing that I was accustomed to using. There were many problems, primarily because different colors of fiber-reactive dyes will not mix. Also as the dye sits, it begins to bond with the water. This makes it impossible to add different colors so fabrics can be timed for shade gradations. After rinsing, I had fabrics that were supposed to be purple coming out blue, and maroons that turned a muddy green.

Then I read about Jan Myers's method of hand dyeing for shade gradations in six to eight individual vats. (To order Jan's booklet, see "Resources.") When I used her method (see below), I discovered that the fiber-reactive dyes do a beautiful job of dyeing cotton fabrics in rich wonderful colors.

Hand-dyeing fabric is not difficult, just time-consuming and tiring when it comes to hauling gallons of water to the garage as I have to do. But there are many good books available on the subject to help you along the way. (See "Resources.") Also, most of the chemical dye suppliers have detailed instructions.

Since these dyes are industrial-type chemicals, precautions, such as covering your face and hands during mixing, are necessary. (A dust mask approved by the National Institute for Occupational Safety and Health is best.) Transferring bagged dyes to screw-top jars for storage is also recommended.

Materials Required for Hand-Dyeing Fabric

One 3-gallon plastic container for each shade gradation
One extra plastic container
Measuring cups and spoons for dyeing purposes only
Rubber gloves
Dust mask
Utensils for stirring
Salt
Soda ash (Arm & Hammer Washing Soda Detergent Booster, blue box)

Sylvia's Recipes for *Facets* Quilt ††

Teal Blue
2 tablespoons brilliant blue
2 tablespoons brilliant green
6 teaspoons black
1½ tablespoons navy blue

Raspberry‡
1 tablespoon maroon
2½ tablespoons brilliant red
1 tablespoon black
1 tablespoon red/brown
1 tablespoon brilliant green

Purple
3 tablespoons brilliant blue
1½ tablespoons brilliant red
3 tablespoons black
2 tablespoons navy blue

Dye pot
2 gallons water (90°)
¾ cup salt (Use either iodized or uniodized, but don't mix the two.)

†† — Recipes are suitable for dyeing 1 yard of fabric.
  Dye names are for Procion® M-Series Fiber-Reactive Dyes. (See "Resources" for ordering information.)

‡ — For RM6 only, you will need to make 2.75 times the recipe for that dye pot and increase the variables for the dye pot accordingly. The time periods for dyeing remain the same.

Jan Myers's Method § for Hand-Dyeing Fabric

1. Before dyeing, wash muslin in hot water with detergent to remove all sizing and oils, and dry for shrinkage.
2. Prepare one dye pot as listed above for each shade gradation desired. Pour salt into dye pot before adding water. Stir to make sure salt is dissolved.
3. While wearing a dust mask, dissolve each dye recipe into 4 cups hot water to make your dye concentrate. Pour the dye concentrate slowly back and forth between two containers to make sure that there are no undissolved lumps.
4. Put 2 cups dye concentrate into the first dye pot for your darkest value. Replace the amount of dye concentrate you took out by adding 2 cups of clear warm water, bringing your dye concentrate back to 4 cups.
5. Stir concentrate, and put 2 cups of the "new" concentrate into the second dye pot. The second pot will have half the color intensity of the first pot. Replace the 2 cups of concentrate with 2 cups of clear warm water and pour 2 cups of this "new" concentrate into the third pot. Continue in this manner, filling dye pots for as many values as you need.
6. While wearing rubber gloves, add wet fabric and submerge entirely in dye pot. Note the time. (For *Facets*, you will add yardages for each shade of bleached and unbleached muslin to each dye pot. For example, for shade 1 of teal blue, add ½ yard of bleached muslin and ½ yard of unbleached muslin.) Stir and rearrange fabric every 10 minutes since the dye has a tendency to settle to the bottom of the container. (Jan has found that the best results are achieved by stirring with your gloved hands.)
7. After 30 minutes, dissolve 3 tablespoons of soda ash in 1 cup of hot water for each dye pot. If there are several dye pots, dissolve soda ash for all dye pots in one large container, i.e., 8 dye pots x 3 tablespoons = 24 tablespoons dissolved in 8 cups of hot water. Add one cup of this solution to each dye pot and stir immediately.
8. Leave fabrics in dye pot for 60 minutes, stirring every 10 minutes.
9. Remove fabrics and rinse with clear, warm water.
10. Wash fabrics in hot water and detergent to remove unreacted dye molecules. At this point, all fabric shade gradations can be washed together. Check the final rinse to make sure that it is absolutely clear. If it is not, repeat the wash process. Dry and press. Fabrics are colorfast and are ready for piecing.

§ — Sylvia incorporated Jan's method to suit her needs for *Facets*, and directions are printed here with Jan's approval.

Ryan's Quilt
1986

Contribute to the merriment of welcoming home a new baby with this heartwarming wall hanging. Sylvia completed *Ryan's Quilt* in four weeks for some friends and their first child. "It was a work of love made for them and their new baby," says Sylvia. "So I quilted hearts all over it." Cross-stitched lambs, ducks, and hearts from The Vanessa-Ann Collection (see "Resources") add more cheer to this special occasion.

Ryan's Quilt

Finished Quilt Size
40" x 40"

Number of Blocks and Finished Size
61 nine-patch blocks—3" x 3"

Fabric Requirements
Lt. blue (LB) — ½ yd.
Med. blue print (MBP) — ½ yd.
Med. blue (MB) — ½ yd.
Rose print (R) — ½ yd.
Dk. blue print (DB) — 1½ yd.
Dk. blue print
  for bias binding — 1 yd.
Backing — 1½ yd.

Number to Cut
Template A — 140 lt. blue
133 rose print
140 med. blue print
176 dk. blue print
Template B — 32 lt. blue
Template C — 24 dk. blue print
Template D — 4 dk. blue print

Cross-stitching Materials
14-count Aida — ½ yd.

DMC
Step 1: Cross-stitch (2 strands).

X	931 antique blue-med.
I	316 antique mauve-med.
∴	930 antique blue-dk.
+	902 garnet-vy.dk.
•	613 drab brown-lt.

Step 2: Backstitch (1 strand).

| ╱ | 931 antique blue-med. |

Quilt Top Assembly
1. Refer to Cross-stitching Charts and make number indicated.

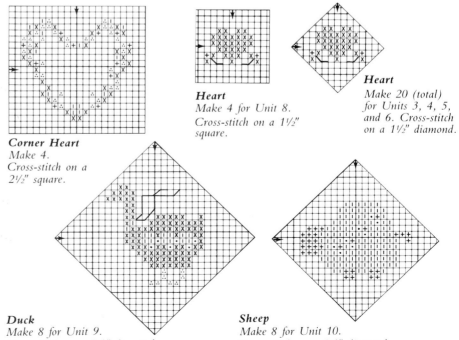

Cross-stitching Charts

Corner Heart
Make 4.
Cross-stitch on a 2½" square.

Heart
Make 4 for Unit 8.
Cross-stitch on a 1½" square.

Heart
Make 20 (total) for Units 3, 4, 5, and 6. Cross-stitch on a 1½" diamond.

Duck
Make 8 for Unit 9.
Cross-stitch on a 2½" diamond.

Sheep
Make 8 for Unit 10.
Cross-stitch on a 2½" diamond.

2. With squares (A), rectangles (B), and cross-stitching squares, make the appropriate number of units, as shown in Color Code Charts for Units. Note placement of cross-stitched squares.

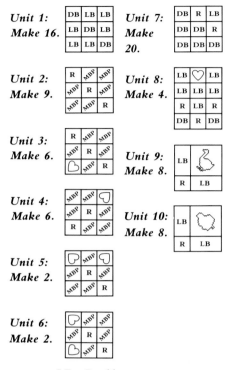

Unit 1:
Make 16.

DB	LB	LB
LB	DB	LB
LB	LB	DB

Unit 7:
Make 20.

DB	R	LB
DB	DB	R
DB	DB	DB

Unit 2:
Make 9.

R	MBP	MBP
MBP	R	MBP
MBP	MBP	R

Unit 8:
Make 4.

LB	♡	LB
LB	LB	LB
R	LB	R
DB	R	DB

Unit 3:
Make 6.

R	MBP	MBP
MBP	R	MBP
♡	MBP	R

Unit 9:
Make 8.

LB	🐇
R	LB

Unit 4:
Make 6.

MBP	MBP	🐇
MBP	R	MBP
R	MBP	MBP

Unit 10:
Make 8.

LB	🦆
R	LB

Unit 5:
Make 2.

🐇	MBP	🐇
MBP	R	MBP
MBP	MBP	R

Unit 6:
Make 2.

🐇	MBP	MBP
MBP	R	MBP
♡	MBP	R

LB—Lt. blue
MBP—Med. blue print
DB—Dk. blue print
R—Rose print

Color Code Charts for Units

3. Referring to Setting Diagram, arrange units as shown. Join units at sides to form rows, adding triangles (C) at each end. Join rectangle (D) to end of unit 8s, triangles (C) to unit 7s as shown, and join to form corner sections. Join rows to complete medallion. Trim outside edges to ¼″ seam allowance.
4. Set medallion on point and cut right triangles from dark blue print for medallion sides. Join bias edges of triangles to sides of medallion.
5. Cut 2 rose print strips, 2 dark blue print strips, and 8 medium blue strips, 1½″ wide, across fabric. Make combination strips of 3 strips each, by joining strips lengthwise as follows: medium blue, rose print, and medium blue; medium blue, dark blue print, and medium blue.
Cut strips, 1½″ wide, across seam lines of joined strips. Join strips, alternating rose print and dark blue

print strips, as shown in Border Piecing Diagram. Make 4 border strips.

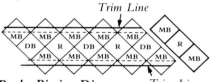

Border Piecing Diagram

Referring to Corner Piecing Diagram, join 1 medium blue square to each end of all 4 strips as shown. In preparation for corner piece, join this square by stitching from outside edge to center seam line and backstitching 1 or 2 stitches. Trim edges of squares to ¼″ seam allowance on top and bottom, as shown in Border Piecing and Corner Piecing Diagrams. Join strips to quilt.
Set cross-stitched heart in each corner. (See Corner Piecing Diagram.) Stitch seam 1, beginning and ending at the seam line and

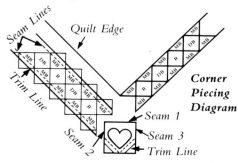

Corner Piecing Diagram

backstitching 1 or 2 stitches at beginning and end. Remove fabric from the machine. Align the raw edges of seam 2 and stitch from the center to the outside edge, backstitching 1 or 2 stitches at the start. Repeat for seam 3. Trim corner edges even with border strips.

Quilting
Quilt in-the-ditch around rose and dark blue print medallion squares. Quilt a feathered heart in each corner. The remainder of the corner area is quilted in a 1″ cross-hatching pattern to blend with the medallion quilting. Quilt in-the-ditch of border squares.

Finished Edges
Bind with a continuous bias strip of dark blue print.

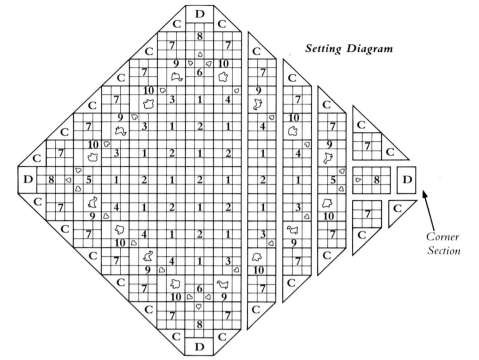

Setting Diagram

Corner Section

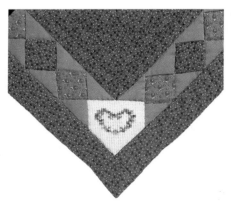

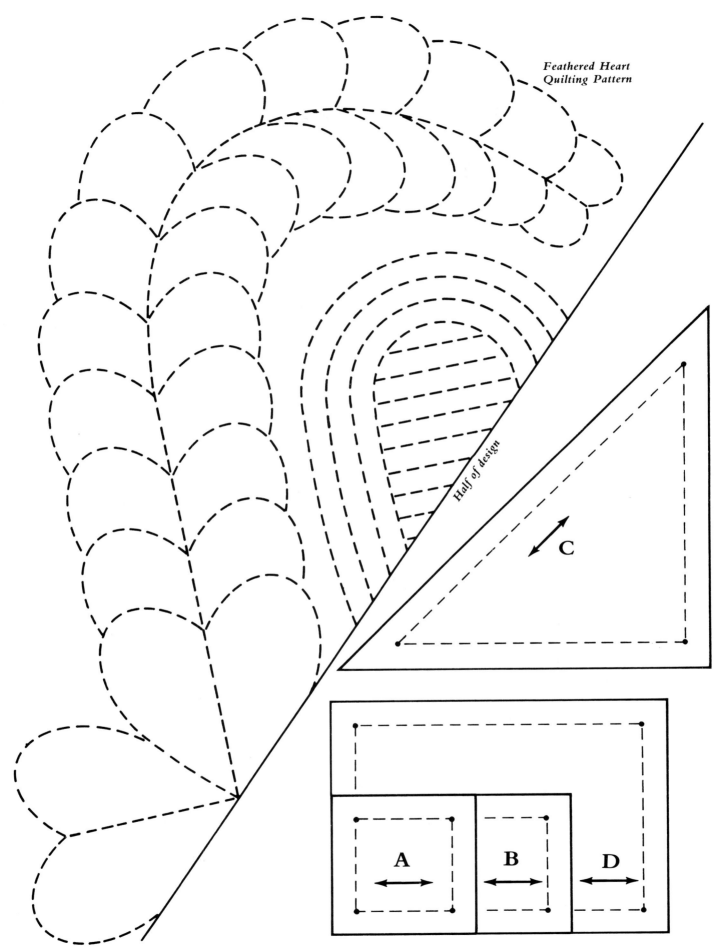

Feathered Heart Quilting Pattern

Half of design

C

A

B

D

TRADITIONS IN QUILTING

Threads linking generations
  intertwine the family tree,
Demand our recollection of a
  childhood memory.
Of kitchen fragrances floating above
  mom's quilting frame,
While underneath, a special place for
  our hide-and-seek game.
By watching mom and granny, I learned
  the quilting art,
A matter of necessity, a matter of the heart.
Aware of my role in our family's
  quilting legacy,
I stitched and pieced the years
  together for my quilting memory.

Broken Star
1936

It was her first job, and the middle of the Depression, but quilting was what occupied her thoughts. At 17, Zelda was captivated by the Star of Bethlehem quilt pattern and decided to make one of her own. "It was my way of relaxing and releasing tension built-up from the daily work load," says Zelda.

Quilting only in the evening hours and without the aid and convenience of today's rotary cutter and strip-piecing techniques, Zelda spent five years producing *Broken Star*. Initially, she copied the quilt from a small picture in a magazine and drafted her own pattern on graph paper. After all the work and effort she put into *Broken Star*, we aren't surprised to hear Zelda say, "I still treasure this as one of my favorite quilts."

Soon after its completion, *Broken Star* won a blue ribbon at the Orange County Fair in Santa Ana, California. And recently, it won another blue ribbon in the Old Quilt Class at the 1984 Pitt County Fair, in Greenville, North Carolina. It seems old quilts never die; they just keep winning ribbons.

Zelda W. Fasciano
Greenville, North Carolina

Observing her mother and grandmothers as they quilted, Zelda fell in love with quilting as a child. "I especially loved the scraps they used—it seemed that each had a story of its own," says Zelda. With their help and a quilt pattern from an elderly neighbor, Zelda made her first quilt. "I began quilting because I was creating something beautiful as I sewed," says Zelda. That was the start of a creative adventure that would remain an integral part of her life.

During the Depression Zelda lived on an Ozark farm, miles from town. "Quilting was the best form of recreation," says Zelda. "And quilting bees were our social events, where we talked and visited." Later, quilting rescued her from hectic days as an office worker, as you will learn in the story about *Broken Star*. When she married and began traveling with her husband, Zelda recalls, "Quilting filled the otherwise lonely moments. Sometimes it helped me to make new friends." And today, Zelda is still making new friends through quilting. "It is an excellent hobby," claims Zelda, "and it keeps me young."

Broken Star

Finished Quilt Size
72" x 83"

Number of Diamonds and Finished Size
32 pieced diamonds—10½" on each side

Fabric Requirements
Yellow	—1 yd.
Hot pink	—1 yd.
Royal blue	—1 yd.
Orange	—1 yd.
Red	—1 yd.
Mint green	—1 yd.
Muslin	—3¾ yd.
Pink for bias binding	—1¼ yd.
Muslin for backing	—4½ yd.

Number to Cut★
Diamond	
	—288 yellow
	256 hot pink
	256 royal blue
	256 orange
	256 red
	256 mint green

★ — Since this is the chapter on traditions, instructions are given as Zelda made the quilt in 1936. We hope rotary cutter and strip-piecing enthusiasts will stop long enough to read and appreciate them.

Quilt Top Assembly
1. Join 7 diamonds at sides to form a strip in the following order from right to left: yellow (Y), mint green (G), red (R), orange (O), royal blue (B), hot pink (P), and yellow (Y).

Diamond Piecing Diagram

Referring to Diamond Piecing Diagram, begin and end the next strip with mint green, keeping the same color order. Begin and end the next strip with red and continue rotating color order in this manner. Make 7 strips.

Match seam lines and join strips to form one large pieced diamond. Make 32 pieced diamonds.

2. Join 8 pieced diamonds at sides to form a star, matching diamond colors and seam lines. (See *Star Piecing Diagram I*.) Sew from the center out and begin and end at seam line. Sew pieced diamonds into quarters; then halves. Periodically check to see that each pair of diamonds forms a 90° angle when joined. Match seam lines of the halves, and sew a few inches across the center. Check to see if seams match. If seams match, sew from center out as before.

Star Piecing Diagram I

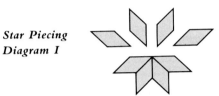

3. To account for any differences in seam allowances, measure the straight edge of each pieced diamond. Add ½″ to this measurement for seam allowances, and cut 8 squares from muslin. Set squares in corners of star. (See *Star Piecing Diagram II*.) With right sides to-

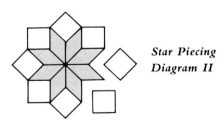

Star Piecing Diagram II

gether, stitch from seam line of outside edge to seam line of inside edge. Stop and backstitch 1 or 2 stitches. Remove fabric from machine. Align the remaining sides and stitch from the center to the seam line of outside edge, backstitching 1 or 2 stitches at the start.

4. Join remaining pieced diamonds into 8 groups of 3, in the same manner as in Step 2. (See *Broken Star* Piecing Diagram I.)

Broken Star *Piecing Diagram I*

5. Set in group diamond sections to sides of muslin squares in same manner as the squares in Step 3. (See *Broken Star* Piecing Diagram II.) Then join pieced diamond sides.

Broken Star *Piecing Diagram II*

6. Measure the straight edge of pieced diamonds, add ¾″, and cut 4 muslin squares. Fold squares on the diagonal, and staystitch ¼″ from either side of diagonal crease. Cut on diagonal and set in triangles to sides, top, and bottom of star corners in the same manner as the squares in Step 3. (See *Broken Star* Piecing Diagram III.)

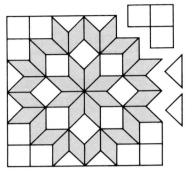

Broken Star *Piecing Diagram III*

7. Measure the straight edge of pieced diamonds as in Step 3, and cut 12 muslin squares. Set squares in corners of stars, as shown in *Broken Star* Piecing Diagram III.

8. Cut 2 border strips, 6″ wide, from muslin and join to top and bottom of quilt.

Quilting
Outline-quilt ¼″ inside all diamond seam lines. Zelda quilted a feathered wreath in each muslin square and a feather pattern in each corner. The remainder of the quilt was quilted in 1″ cross-hatching.

Finished Edges
Bind with a continuous bias strip of pink fabric.

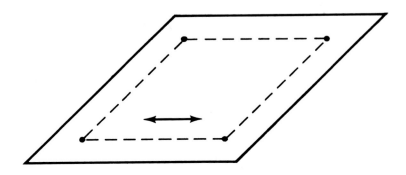

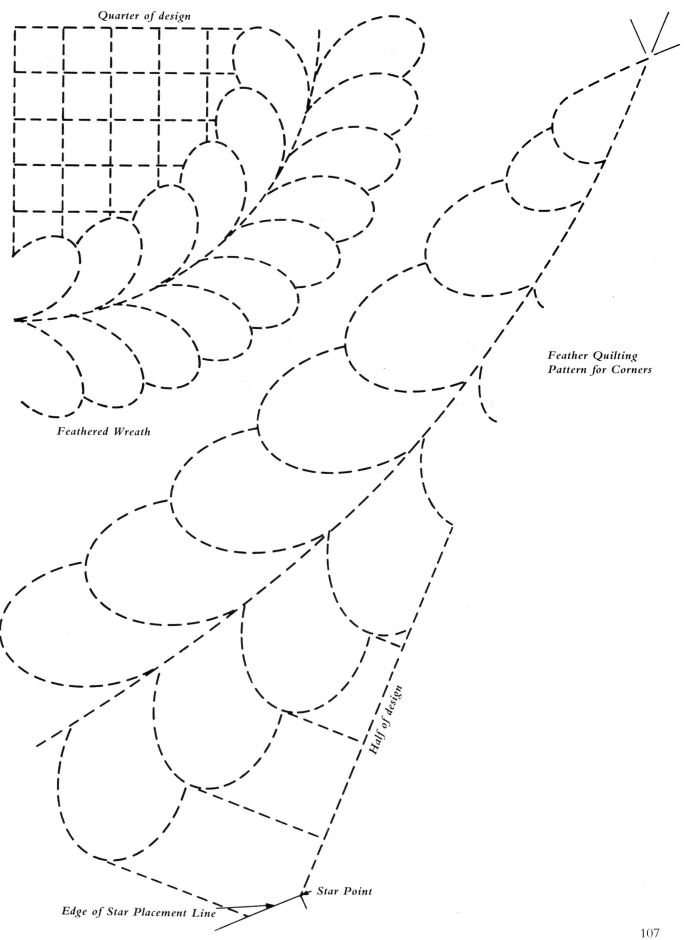

Quarter of design

Feather Quilting
Pattern for Corners

Feathered Wreath

Half of design

Star Point

Edge of Star Placement Line

Lucy McVey Bush

New Port Richey, Florida

"It's like candy to me," says Lucy, "to see something so beautiful." That's what it's like for Lucy when she removes a quilt from its frame. Lucy grew up in a quilting environment and witnessed first-hand the value of quilting. Her mother, Iona, was well-known for her quilting, so much so that she would often receive mail simply addressed to The Quilter. "Mother never let her hands idle," recalls Lucy. "Quilting provided part of our livelihood on the family farm."

"My first experience with quilting was learning to make a nine-patch," says Lucy. "Mother set the patches, and we quilted them."

Lucy, being the only daughter, inherited her mother's quilts, quilt tops, and a suitcase full of quilting patterns. "I am still pulling patterns from that old suitcase," says Lucy. "Many can't be found in any store today." Lucy hopes to complete many of her mother's unfinished quilts and cherishes each one. "I just can't part with them," says Lucy. "Family memories reside in every one of them."

Today, Lucy and her daughter Wilma share many hours making quilts. With Wilma doing most of the piecing and Lucy, the quilting, somehow we know Iona would be pleased.

First Step
Pieced 1890s
Quilted 1964–1974

First Step places the first stepping stone of a trail that travels through the generations of Lucy's family. Lucy's grandmother Alice Littleton quilted for many years and reached a time when she grew tired of using the same quilt patterns. One day while her husband, Joe, was laid up with a broken foot, Alice asked, "Joe, since you can't do any farm chores now, will you design a new quilt pattern for me?" He obliged her and said that he would call it *First Step* for two reasons. First, because designing this pattern was the first thing he did to get himself on the road to recovery. And secondly, he believed that Alice would have the blocks pieced by the time he was able to throw away his crutches and take his first steps.

She did, and several years later Alice gave the blocks to one of her daughters, Iona Littleton McVey (Lucy's mother). Iona stored the blocks for many years, but eventually joined them and started the quilting in 1964. Midway through the quilting, Iona passed away. Sometime later, over eighty years after the first stitch was made, Lucy took the last stitch on *First Step*.

This early 1900s photograph shows Lucy's grandfather, Joseph Littleton, who was designer of First Step, *with his family in front of their farmhouse in Kentucky. They are* (left to right)—*Nancy Easton Heflin (Lucy's great-grandmother), Iona Littleton (Lucy's mother), Datie Littleton (Iona's sister), Joseph Littleton, Stella Littleton (Iona's youngest sister), Alice Littleton (Lucy's grandmother), Lula Littleton (Iona's eldest sister), and Iona's twin sisters, Ida and Ita Littleton.*

First Step

Finished Quilt Size
74" x 89"

Number of Blocks and Finished Size
30 First Step blocks—10" x 10"

Fabric Requirements
Maroon prints	—1⅞ yd. total
White prints	—2 yd. total
Peach	—2½ yd.
Muslin for bias binding	—1¼ yd.
Backing	—5 yd.

Number to Cut
Template A	— 240 maroon prints
Template B	— 120 white prints
Template C	— 150 white prints
Template D	— 120 maroon prints

Quilt Top Assembly
1. Referring to Block Piecing Diagram I, join triangles (A) to sides of square (C). Make 3 pieced triangles. Join pieced triangle to triangle (B) to form a square. Make 3 small pieced squares.

Join rectangle (D) to side of 1 small pieced square. Join end of rectangle (D) to side of square (C). Referring to Block Piecing Diagram I, join strip to form a large pieced square.

Join triangles (A, B), square (C), and rectangles (D) to form corner section.

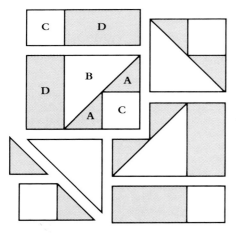

Block Piecing Diagram I

2. Join small pieced squares to sides of corner section, as shown in Block Piecing Diagram II.

Set in pieced square. Begin stitching from the outside edge of one side and stitch up to the seam line. Stop and backstitch 1 or 2 stitches.

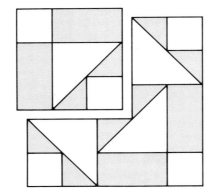

Block Piecing Diagram II

Setting Diagram   **FS = First Step Block**

Remove fabric from the machine. Align the remaining sides and stitch from the center to the outside edge, backstitching 1 or 2 stitches at the start. Make 30 blocks.

3. Cut twenty 10½" squares, 18 right-angled triangles with 10½" sides, and 4 corner triangles from peach. Set pieced blocks on the diagonal and alternate with solid squares, as shown in Setting Diagram. Join into diagonal rows, adding triangles to ends as shown. Join rows.

Quilting
Lucy quilted horizontal parallel lines, 1" apart, across each pieced block and a feathered wreath in solid squares and triangles.

Finished Edges
Bind with a continuous bias strip of muslin.

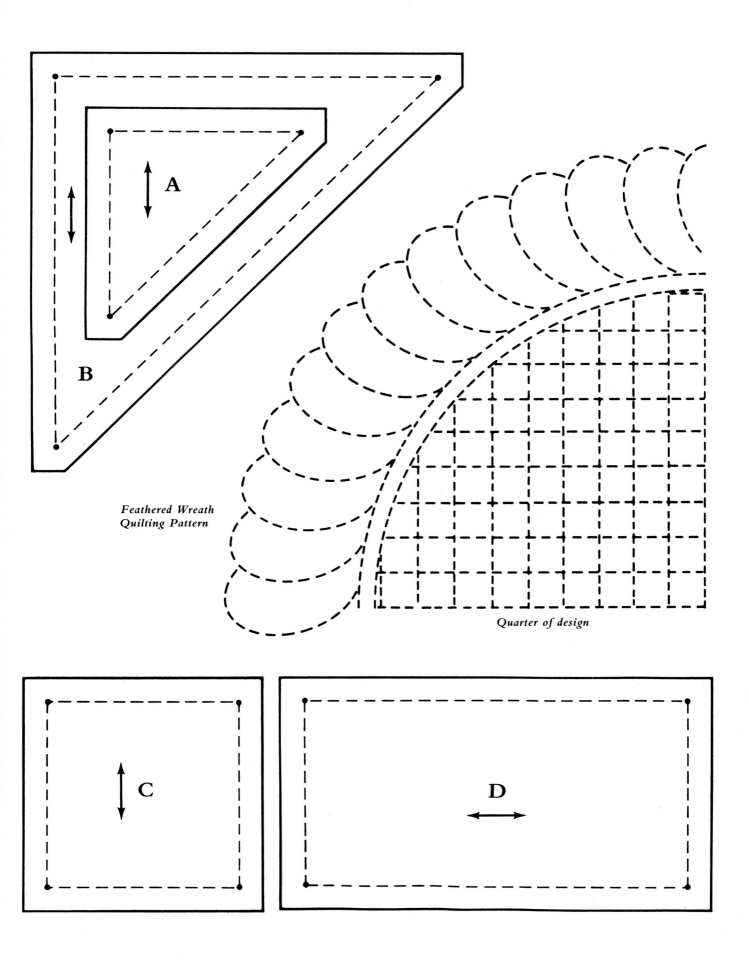

A

B

Feathered Wreath
Quilting Pattern

Quarter of design

C

D

Mary Jo & Leonard Jackson

Estill Springs, Tennessee

Appreciation of and admiration for quilts and quilters have always been a part of Mary Jo and Leonard's family life. She learned to quilt as a child by watching her mother, but Mary Jo couldn't seriously undertake quiltmaking until she retired several years ago. "It's a great hobby and good therapy," says Mary Jo, who especially enjoys sharing her quilting expertise with the individuals at a local senior citizens' center.

Since Estill Springs's last big snowstorm, Mary Jo has boasted of the satisfaction quilting brings to her family. While the snow was piling up outside, her husband, Leonard, caught a severe case of cabin fever and couldn't help noticing how content his wife was with her quilting. "Looks like you're having such a good time quilting," he said to her. "How about letting me help you?" Without hesitation, she grabbed her scraps and sat him down in front of the sewing machine. Needless to say, the snow melted before he finished the top, and Mary Jo lost her quilting partner to other endeavors. But she and the senior citizens' group were happy to quilt it for him.

Decades before, Leonard's mother did much the same thing when ten-year-old Leonard was getting underfoot. She plopped some squares of fabric in his lap, handed him a needle and thread, and kept him busy hand-piecing four-patch blocks for a Bird in the Window pattern. The blocks were set by his mother and later quilted by his sister. Today, Leonard's spare time is filled with making quilt racks and quilting frames.

Sunflower
1900s

Rows of glorious sunflowers keep smiling for generations of Coop and Jackson family members. If quilts could talk, *Sunflower* might tell us of being carefully pieced by the loving hands of Mary Jo's great-grandmother Virginia Webb Coop. And dare we ask *Sunflower* to share the juicy tidbits of "information" that were heard while the ladies from Moore County, Tennessee, deftly placed their quilting stitches upon her flower heads?

In the years to follow, *Sunflower* covered a bed or two at Mary Jo's grandmother's house and then went on to cover another at her Uncle Arthur's home. Sometime after Uncle Arthur died, *Sunflower* was given to Mary Jo by Uncle Arthur's widow, Myrtle, in gratitude for Mary Jo's staying with her after Uncle Arthur's death. Now, *Sunflower* rests contentedly among a multitude of family quilts.

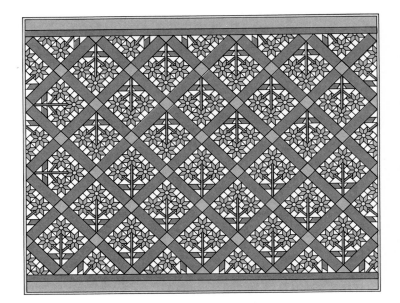

Sunflower

Finished Quilt Size
82" x 102"

Number of Blocks and Finished Size
27 Sunflower blocks—11" x 11"
15 Half-Sunflower blocks
2 Quarter-Sunflower blocks

Fabric Requirements
Orange — 4 yd.
Bright orange — ⅜ yd.
Green — 4¼ yd.
Muslin — 3¾ yd.
Bright orange
   for bias binding — 1¼ yd.
Backing — 6 yd.

Number to Cut
Template A — 840 orange
Template B — 402 muslin
Template C — 456 muslin
Template D — 27 muslin
Template E — 35 green
Template E★ — 35 green
Template F — 27 muslin
Template G — 27 muslin
Template H — 27 long green
         stems
         35 short green
         stems
Template H★ — 35 short green
         stems
Template I — 15 orange
Template J — 114 bright
         orange
Template K — 16 muslin
Template L — 16 muslin
         2 orange
Template M — 16 muslin
★ — Flip or turn over template if fabric is one-sided.

Quilt Top Assembly
1. Join sides of 8 diamonds (A), as shown in Sunflower Piecing Diagram. Stitch all seams from and to seam lines. Join diamonds into quarters; then halves. Match seam

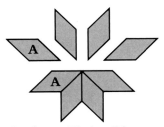

Sunflower Piecing Diagram

lines of the halves and join. Make 3 sunflowers.

Set squares (B) and triangles (C) between diamonds, as shown in Sunflower Block Piecing Diagram.

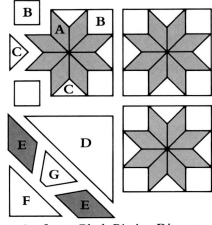

Sunflower Block Piecing Diagram

Stitch one side of square (B) or triangle (C) to one side of diamond (A). Begin stitching from the outside edge and stitch up to the seam line. Stop and backstitch 1 or 2 stitches. Remove fabric from the machine. Align the remaining sides and stitch from the center to the outside edge, backstitching 1 or 2 stitches at the start. Make 3 Sunflower squares. Join pieces (D, E, F, and G), as shown in Sunflower Block Piecing Diagram. Join pieced squares at sides to form 2 rows. Join rows to complete Sunflower block. Make 27 blocks.

2. Appliqué stems (H) and centers (J) to each block. (See Sunflower Block Appliqué Diagram.) To aid in appliquéing stems and centers, machine-stitch on seam line before turning fabric under.

Sunflower Block Appliqué Diagram

3. Referring to the Half-Sunflower Block Piecing Diagram, make 8 half blocks as shown and 7 the mirror image of these. (See quilt drawing.) Appliqué stem (H) and centers (J) to blocks. Trim center (J), as shown, even with seam allowance.

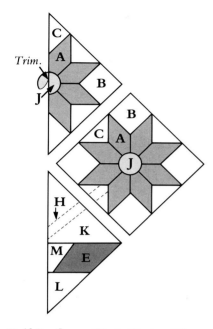

Half-Sunflower Block Piecing Diagram

4. Referring to Quarter-Sunflower Block Piecing Diagrams, make 1 each as shown. Appliqué stem (H) and centers (J), as before, to blocks. Trim centers (J) even with seam allowance.

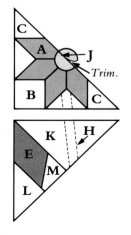

Quarter-Sunflower Block Piecing Diagrams

5. Cut 70 sashing strips, 3¾″ wide, from green. Set Sunflower blocks on the diagonal and arrange, as shown in quilt drawing. Join sashing strips to opposite sides of Sunflower blocks to form diagonal rows, as shown in Setting Diagram.

6. Cut twenty-seven 3¾″ accent squares from orange. Alternate accent squares with the remaining sashing strips to form sashing rows. Join triangle (I or L) to the ends of each sashing row, as shown in Setting Diagram. Join sashing rows to Sunflower block rows.

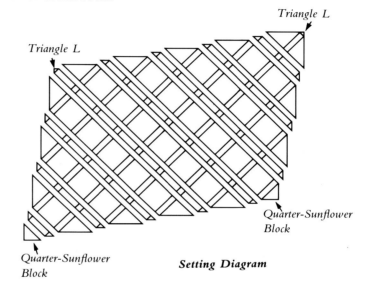

Setting Diagram

7. Cut 2 border strips, 2½″ wide, from green and join to sides of quilt.

8. Cut 2 border strips, 3¾″ wide, from orange and join to sides of quilt.

Quilting
Outline-quilt ¼″ inside all seam lines of Sunflower block. Quilt diagonal parallel lines, ½″ apart, on sashing strips. Outline-quilt ¼″ inside seam lines of sashing squares and triangles (I and L). Quilt straight lines from corner to corner of accent squares to form a large *X*. Quilt parallel lines, ½″ apart, the length of the green border strips and, ¾″ apart, the length of the orange border strips.

Finished Edges
Bind with a continuous bias strip of bright orange fabric.

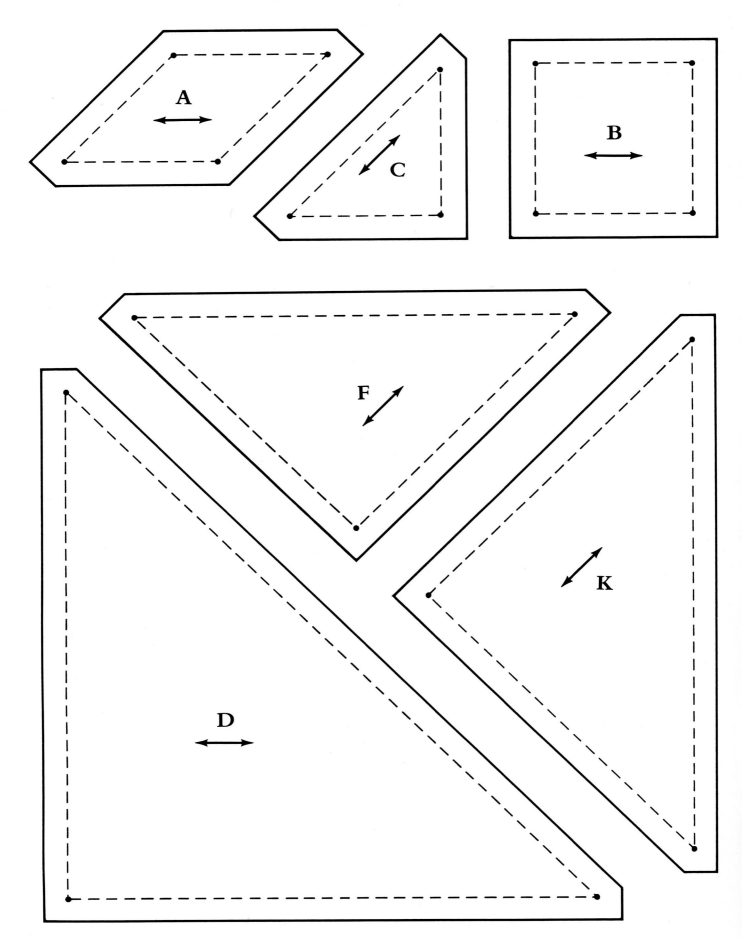

BEE QUILTERS

Many hands, many stitches,
Generous hearts, tireless ambitions.
Abundant talent, shared skills,
Joyous laughter, pleasant thrills.
Dear friends, iced cakes,
Smiling spirits, coffee breaks.
Gathering together, working for free,
What could it be but a quilting bee!

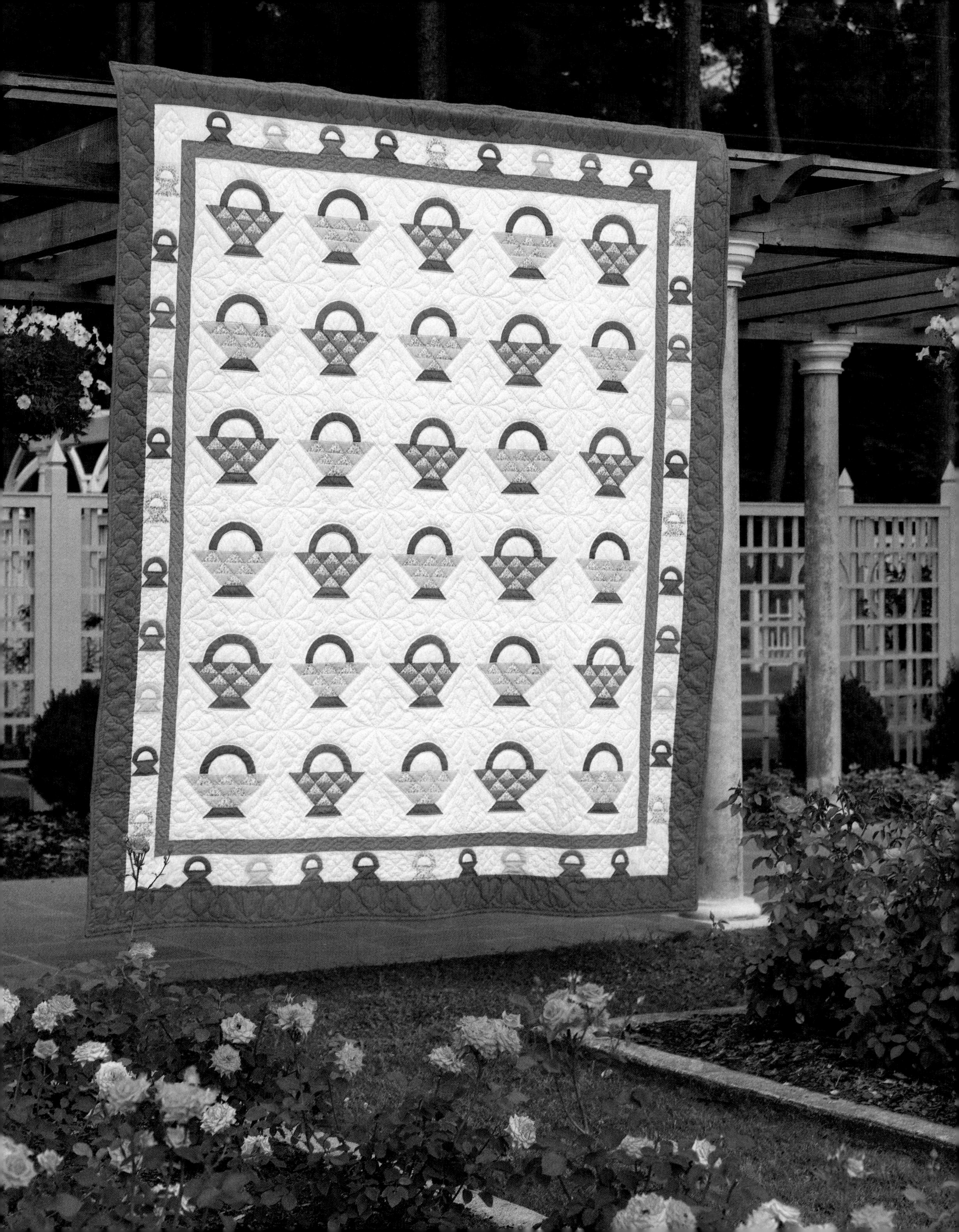

Cobblestone Quilter's Guild

Charleston, South Carolina

Not far from the echo of cobblestone streets, these Charleston quilters perpetuate the art of quilting, practiced so frequently by the city's early settlers. Monthly quilt-related programs, workshops, and show-and-tell sessions keep the quilting tradition alive among guild members.

Only four years from its beginning, the Cobblestone Quilter's Guild boasts over 100 dedicated quilters. Members are especially proud of the many philanthropic gifts they can make because of their quilting activities. Proceeds from raffle quilts are divided among various charities, such as senior citizens' programs, libraries and museums, and a shelter for abused women and children.

Basket Quilt
1985

Quilted hearts and perfectly aligned postage stamp baskets frame stacks of springtime baskets. "The *Basket Quilt* was truly a group effort," says former guild President, Darra Duffy. Over 60 Basket-block kits were pieced by individual members. Once blocks were pieced and the top was completed, the quilt was transported while in frame to several members' homes where it was quilted on a drop-in basis. "This way," explains Darra, "everyone had a chance to quilt."

Some of the quilters for *Basket Quilt* were Ellen Anson, Mary Ann Calhoun, Eldeen Carter, Laura Chapman, Nancy Davidson, Darra Duffy, Kimberly Gibson, Margaret Harrison, Ruth McIver, Nancy Rignel, Brenda Rollins, Susan Runge, Kristin Steiner, and Nan Tournier.

Basket Quilt

Finished Quilt Size
92" x 110"

Number of Blocks and Finished Size
30 Basket blocks—10" x 10"

Fabric Requirements

Rose with white pin dots★	— 2⅝ yd.
Yellow print	— 1 yd.
Floral print	— 1⅛ yd.
Olive green	— 3¼ yd.
Blue	— 1⅛ yd
Cream	— 5⅞ yd.
Olive green for bias binding	— 1¼ yd.
Backing	— 8¼ yd.

★ — Throughout the directions, rose with white pin dots will be designated as rose.

Number to Cut

Template A	—	135 rose
		135 yellow print
		180 floral print
		45 olive green
		45 blue
Template B	—	16 rose
		16 yellow print
		16 floral print
		16 olive green
		16 blue
		80 cream
Template C	—	8 rose
		8 yellow print
		8 floral print
		8 olive green
		8 blue
Template D	—	8 rose
		8 yellow print
		8 floral print
		8 olive green
		8 blue
Template E	—	15 olive green
		15 blue
Template F	—	40 cream
Template G	—	30 cream
Template H	—	60 cream
Template I	—	30 cream
4½" squares	—	36 cream
10½" squares	—	20 cream
Right triangles	—	18 cream with 10" finished sides
		4 cream with 10" finished bias (hypotenuse)

Quilt Top Assembly

1. Referring to the Basket Block Piecing Diagram, join 9 rose triangles (A), 6 floral triangles (A), and 1 olive green triangle (A) in rows. Join rows to complete basket body. Join cream rectangles (H) and olive green triangles (A), as shown in Basket Block Piecing Diagram and join to sides of basket body.

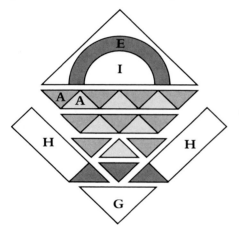

Basket Block Piecing Diagram

Center olive green basket handle (E) on cream triangle (I) and appliqué. Join cream triangle (I) to basket top and cream triangle (G) to basket bottom to complete Basket block. Make 15 with rose, floral print, and olive green fabrics. Make 15 with yellow print, floral print, and blue fabrics.

2. Set Basket blocks on the diagonal, and alternate basket colors, as shown in quilt photograph. Refer to Setting Diagram and join Basket blocks, squares, and right triangles into diagonal strips. Join strips.

Setting Diagram   **BB = Basket Block**

3. Cut 4 border strips, 2½″ wide, from rose. Join to quilt and miter corners.

4. Join yellow print triangles (B) to cream triangles (B), as shown in Border Basket Piecing Diagram. Join them to yellow print triangle (C). Center yellow print basket handle (D) on cream rectangle (F) and appliqué. Join rectangle to basket top to complete Border Basket block. Make 8 Border Basket blocks with each of the fabrics except cream, for a total of 40.

Border Basket Piecing Diagram

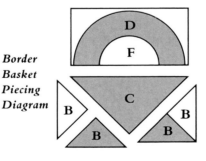

5. Referring to quilt photograph for basket color order, alternate 9 Border Basket blocks with 8 cream 4½″ squares. Join at *sides* for top border strip. Make 1 more border strip for bottom.

6. Referring to quilt photograph for basket color order, alternate 11 Border Basket blocks with 10 cream 4½″ squares. Join at tops and bottoms for side border strip. Make a strip for each side.

7. Center and pin a strip to one side and the top. Measure the distance needed to join strips and form mitered corners. Cut corner pieces from cream, remembering to add seam allowances. (You may want to do this with the remaining strips to assure accurate cutting measurements.) Unpin strips and join corner pieces to strip ends. Join strips to quilt and miter corners.

8. Cut 4 border strips, 6″ wide, from olive green. Join to quilt and miter corners.

Quilting

Outline-quilt inside seam line of floral print triangles. Outline-quilt ¼″ inside seam line of cream triangle (G), rectangles (H), and basket base. Outline-quilt ¼″ outside basket handle seam line. The Cobblestone Quilters quilted a rope pattern along the rose border strip and a plume pattern in each large cream square and triangle.

For pieced border, quilt the double quatrefoil pattern in each 4″ cream square. Outline-quilt outside seam line of each basket handle and ¼″ inside seam line of basket shape.

For outside border, hearts are quilted, alternating top and bottom positions.

Finished Edges

Bind with a continuous bias strip of olive green fabric.

Half of design

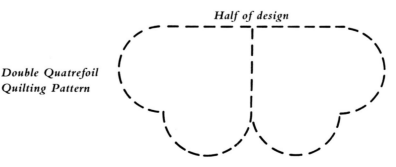

Double Quatrefoil Quilting Pattern

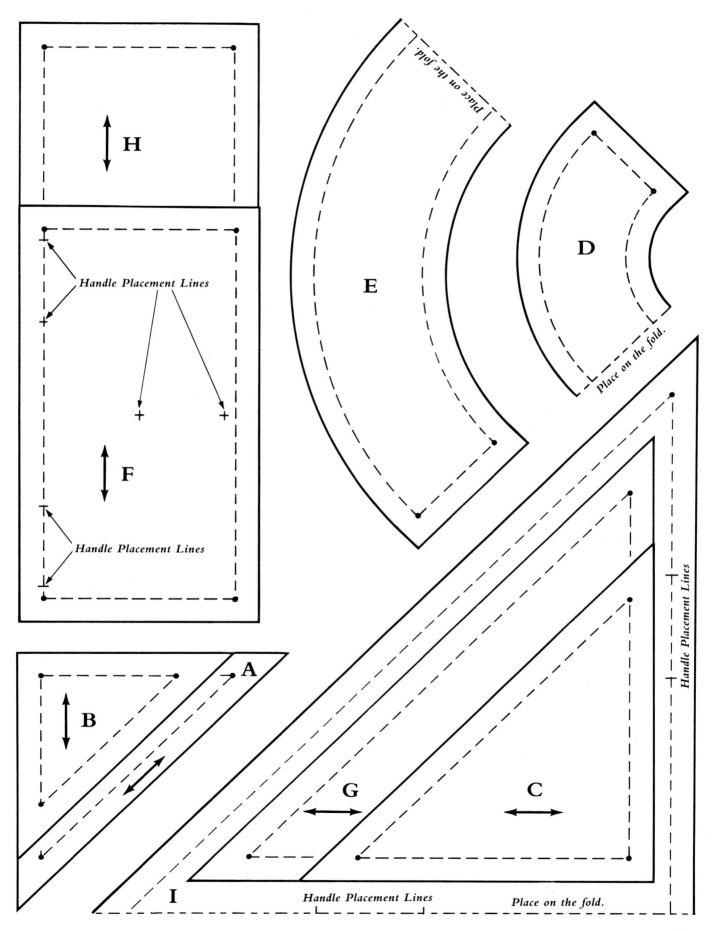

H

Handle Placement Lines

Handle Placement Lines

F

Place on the fold.

E

D

Place on the fold.

Handle Placement Lines

A

B

I

G

C

Handle Placement Lines

Place on the fold.

Representing the many hardworking and dedicated quilters of the Golden Triangle Guild are (seated, left to right)—Pearl McEachern and Kay Figart; (standing, left to right)—Anita Murphy and Norma Clubb.

Golden Triangle Quilt Guild

Beaumont, Texas

Quilters from 23 neighboring Texas and Louisiana cities compose the membership of the Golden Triangle Quilt Guild. "Because of the guild, most of us have become very good friends with people we would never have known," says guild president, Norma Clubb. To accommodate the different schedules of nearly 170 members, the guild conducts afternoon and evening meetings with the same format on the third Thursday of each month.

The guild's monthly newsletter, *The Pieceful Times,* keeps everyone abreast of the newest quilt books, quilt exhibits, and competitions, and includes a pinch of quilting history.

Quilting demonstrations by members are regularly held in school libraries so that children can observe quiltmaking and visit with the quilters. Quilts made by the guild have been auctioned for a national telethon and a local art museum. Two quilts have been donated to the Ronald McDonald House in Houston.

Says guild founder, Anita Murphy, "Some quilters have loved our meetings so much that they actually learned to drive so they would not have to miss one or depend on someone else to take them. Seeing so many women taking up this marvelous art form is really a lasting reward."

Spring Amish
1986

Spring Amish gloriously displays the precious scraps and stitches of 86 Golden Triangle Quilt Guild members. "I wanted a quilt that would get as many involved as possible," said quilt originator and project organizer, Anita Murphy. "A project that gets nearly everyone to participate is one of the greatest." With so many members living in all directions from Beaumont, Texas, this reversible quilt-as-you-go block was ideal.

Golden Triangle Quilt Guild members who participated in the making of *Spring Amish* are as follows: Renella Babin, Dorothy Beard, Marge Bieber, Lynn Brown, Marge Campbell, Robin Campbell, Dolores Carpenter, Sandra Chain, Marti Childress, Norma Clubb, Anne Charlotte Collins, Dot Collins, Helen Cox, Cathron Deutsch, Cecelia Ewald, Margaret Ezer, Annie Franklin, Mavis Franklin, Kay Figart, Gloria Gaar, Vivian Godkin, Elizabeth Gulley, Louise Hamilton, Frances Hanks, Ellen Harris, Frances Heard, Pat Hebert, Nishie Holiday, Florence Hollier, Pearl Hoot, Happy James, Georgenia Jaschke, Robbie Jenan, Isabel Johann, Mable Johnson, Zena Standifer Johnson, Betty Johnston, Peggy Jones, Jerry Kelley, Dean Kuebodeaux, Catherine Kuhl, Sally Lanasa, Lotus LaRocca, Vicki Leeper, Louise Leubstorff, Nell Linscomb, Barbara Loden, Peggy Martin, Viola Mason, Laverne Mathews, Linda Mathews, Beverly McClintock, Noel Ann McCord, Yvonne McDaniel, Pearl McEachern, Thelma McGee, Joyce Montgomery, Juno Mulder, Annie Muller, Anita Murphy, Denise Nevils, Lou O'Quinn, Jerry Parker, Medy Patricia, Martha Petroelje, Mary Ray, Sharon Richardson, Evelyn Roberts, Easter Rouen, Mary Rudduck, Betty Schultz, Dottie Smith, Pauline Smith, Ruth Stecher, Annie Mae Stringer, Charlene Stringer, Silvia Sturrock, Linda Taliaferro, Carol Taylor, Merle Vincent, Addie Wallace, Barbara Wallace, Delma Weiler, Sylvia Weir, Cynthia Weller, and Mildred White.

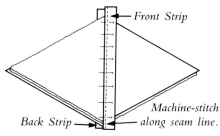

Spring Amish (reversible)·

Finished Quilt Size
100″ x 120″

**Number of Blocks and
Finished Size**
120 reversible blocks—10″ x 10″

Fabric Requirements

Pastel scrap prints	—20 yd. total
Blue print for piecing and binding	—6½ yd.
Muslin	—8 yd.

Quilt Top Assembly

1. Cut sixty 11″ squares from blue print. Cut only 3 squares per row and save the leftover strip of fabric for binding. Cut squares along the diagonal to make 120 triangles.

2. Cut sixty 11″ squares from muslin. Cut only 3 squares per row as before and save the leftover strip for sashing. Cut squares along the diagonal to make 120 triangles.

3. Cut one hundred and twenty 11″ squares of batting.

4. Cut two strips, 1½″ wide, from scrap fabrics to go across the diagonal of the block. (Cut each with generous length that can easily be trimmed after attaching.) On the back of each strip, mark a ¼″ seam allowance on one side.

5. Referring to Block Piecing Diagram I, pin the blue print triangle to the front of a batting square and the muslin triangle to the back on the opposite end.

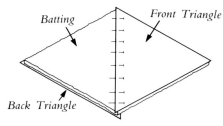

Block Piecing Diagram I

Pin each scrap strip to the triangles (front and back), as shown in Block Piecing Diagram II. Seam lines should match on both sides. Machine-stitch through the five layers. This is the hidden seam and must be accurate, or the rest of the block will be out of line.

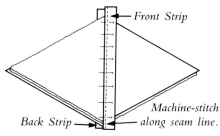

Block Piecing Diagram II

6. Work on one side at a time. All strips are 1½″ wide with seam allowance. (For our purposes, we

will begin on the front.) On the front, finger-press the first strip toward batting. Pin second strip to first strip, batting, and back triangle. Be sure to pin the first strip on the back out of the way so it does not get caught in the second row of stitching. (Anita recommends that you always finger-press strips before cutting the length. If you cut the strip before finger-pressing, it will be too short.)

Stitch through all four layers. This stitching will be the quilting for the back triangle so you may want to join these strips by h nd.. (Anita reminds you to stitch a. straight a seam line as possible, that your quilting rows on the t will be neat and straight.)

Eight strips in all are added in this manner to the front of the block.

7. Now turn to the back and repeat. Make 120 blocks.

8. Before setting blocks, make a master template 10½″ square. Use this to trim blocks to a uniform size before joining.

Arrange blocks in 12 rows of 10 blocks each, as shown in quilt photograph. Cut a sashing strip, 2″ x 10½″, from muslin. Fold in half lengthwise and press. With right sides facing and the muslin strip on top, join blocks together at sides. (See Row Assembly Diagram I.) Appliqué folded free edge of muslin sashing strip to block, as shown in Row Assembly Diagram II. Make 12 rows.

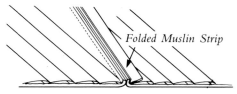

Row Assembly Diagram I

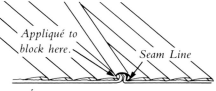

Row Assembly Diagram II

9. Join rows with muslin strips the length of each row in the same manner as in Step 8.

Finished Edges
Bind with blue print fabric.

Birmingham Quilter's Guild

Birmingham, Alabama

In the spring of 1978, an avid quilter placed an ad in a small local newspaper, calling all quilters. Six ladies responded, and the Birmingham Quilter's Guild was born. By word of mouth, advertisements, newsletters, quilt demonstrations, and displays, membership in the guild grew to 41 by the end of the first year.

Today, the guild has over 80 members and is still growing, due in part to their dedication to all facets of quiltmaking. Members are encouraged to participate in monthly hands-on workshops to sharpen quilting skills and/or learn the latest techniques.

Monies received from guild dues and the annual quilt raffle finance quilting demonstrations for children, craft and community festivals, book donations to the local library, and scholarships for quilting seminars and workshops.

Maple Leaf
1985

Maple leaves glittering in this salutatory stance remind us throughout the year of the beauty of autumn. In six months guild members, under the direction of chairperson Martha McDonald, hand-pieced blocks, assembled rows of diagonal sashing, and quilted a lattice framework to construct this spectrum of maple leaf radiance.

"Blocks were produced in a workshop setting to teach the basics of hand-piecing," says Martha, "and the scrap bag effect came as a result of each member contributing her own choice of print." Thirty-two different blocks were selected for the quilt, based on the overall color balance and value, to produce the best setting.

Some of the quilters for *Maple Leaf* were Ray Anderson, Helen Cain, Judy Cloe, Rosemary Cole, Gwen Cox, Pauline Darche, Nell Dumas, Marty Duncan, Dot Ellis, Leslie Galla, Nell Howell, Leigh Marlow, Laurie McAnulty, Martha McDonald, Sherrie Reynolds, Erma Scudder, Sara Self, Susan Seng, Nonee Siergiej, Aldine Thomas, Jean Vance, and Mary Weinschreider.

Maple Leaf

Finished Quilt Size
84" x 101"

Number of Blocks and Finished Size
32 blocks—9" x 9"

Fabric Requirements
Scrap prints★

Brown/rusts	— ¾ yd.
Yellow/golds	— ½ yd.
Greens	— ½ yd.
Red/oranges	— ½ yd.
Off-whites	— ½ yd.
Dark green	—3⅞ yd.
Muslin	—2¼ yd.
Rust print	—3 yd.
Rust print for bias binding	—1¼ yd.
Backing	—5¾ yd.

★ — Scrap yardage for a Maple Leaf block is a 4" x 24" rectangle.

Number to Cut

Template A	—33 brown/rusts
	21 yellow/golds
	21 greens
	12 red/oranges
	9 off-whites
	64 muslin
Template B	—44 brown/rusts
	28 yellow/golds
	28 greens
	16 red/oranges
	12 off-whites
	128 muslin
Template C	—11 brown/rusts
	7 yellow/golds
	7 greens
	4 red/oranges
	3 off-whites

Quilt Top Assembly

1. Place stem piece (C) on the diagonal of muslin square (A) and appliqué. Join scrap print triangles (B) with muslin triangles (B), as shown in Block Piecing Diagram. Join pieced squares with squares (A) to form 3 rows. Join rows. Make 32 Maple Leaf blocks.

To save time, string-piece all muslin triangles (B) to scrap triangles (B). Set aside, and use them as needed for each block.

2. Using color balance and value as criteria, arrange Maple Leaf blocks

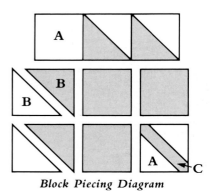

Block Piecing Diagram

in diagonal rows, as shown in Setting Diagrams.

Cut 40 sashing strips, 2½" x 9½", from dark green. Join sashing strips to opposite sides of Maple Leaf blocks to form rows, as shown in Setting Diagram I.

3. Cut nine sashing strips, 2½" wide, from dark green to attach to block rows. Join to one side of 8 block rows, as shown in Setting Diagram I. (The longest sashing strip will be joined to rows at the final assembly of the quilt top.)

4. Cut 14 right triangles from muslin for ends of block rows. Join to each end of block rows to form row units. (See Setting Diagram I.)

Cut 2 right triangles from muslin for corner units and complete corner unit assembly, as shown in Setting Diagram I.

5. Begin with corner unit and join row units. (See Setting Diagram II.) Cut 2 right triangles from muslin for remaining corners and join to quilt.

6. Cut 4 border strips, 4½" wide, from dark green, join to quilt, and miter corners.

7. Cut 4 border strips, 6½" wide, from rust print, join to quilt, and miter corners.

Quilting

Outline-quilt along seam lines of Maple Leaf block. Quilt a 1" cross-hatching pattern on large muslin triangles. Quilt parallel diagonal lines at a 45° angle, 3½" apart, on green and rust print borders.

Finished Edges

Bind with a continuous bias strip of rust print fabric.

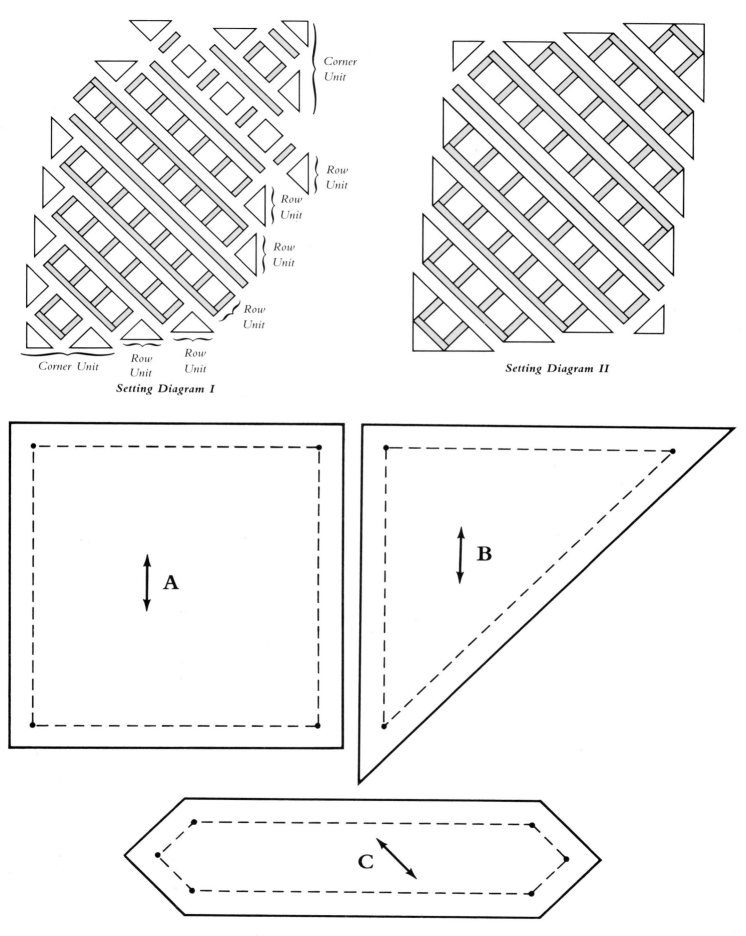

Corner Unit

Row Unit

Row Unit

Row Unit

Row Unit

Corner Unit   *Row Unit*   *Row Unit*

Setting Diagram I

Setting Diagram II

A

B

C

129

Sunburst and Ribbons
1986

Wrap a little sunshine with flamboyant festoons of appliquéd ribbons and bows. The Quilters admit that *Sunburst and Ribbons* contains the most extensive appliqué that they have ever done, but their success has stimulated them to select more complex appliqué patterns for future quilts.

The pattern and fabrics were chosen by Marie Chabot. Members who worked on *Sunburst and Ribbons* were Marie Chabot, Peg Crosby, Dorothy Graham, Alice Grenier, Marge Johnson, Florence Lavallee, Janet Manahan, Dorothy Oles, Joan Reece, Eileen Siegel, Mary Slocum, and Sally Stevenson.

The Quilters take a break from quilting just long enough to have their picture taken. They are (seated, left to right)—Florence Lavallee, Sally Stevenson, Dorothy Oles, Marge Johnson, Alice Grenier, and Janet Manahan, and (standing, left to right)—Eileen Siegel, Dorothy Graham, Marie Chabot, Joan Reece, and Mary Slocum.

The Quilters

Sutton, Massachusetts

The Quilters of Sutton, Massachusetts, credit the six-year success of their group to its informal structure. Meeting every Tuesday for quilting, this group of 12 travel to a different member's home each week on a volunteer basis so that all can remain flexible in their commitments. "Our quilting is recreational rather than another appointment to keep," explains The Quilters' spokeswoman, Janet Manahan.

Quilts are made in an assembly-line fashion. A few members quilt on one quilt, while others begin hand-piecing the next. This allows members to participate in the quiltmaking area they enjoy most.

Their first quilt was made for a church fund-raiser, and since then, they have made six quilts for group members. As Janet explains, "We are diverse in many ways, but quilting is the interest that has made us friends."

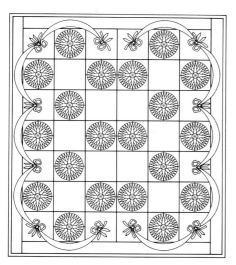

Sunburst and Ribbons

Finished Quilt Size
92" x 105"

Number of Blocks and Finished Size
20 Sunburst blocks—13½" x 13½"

Fabric Requirements

Purple floral print	—3 yd.
Green	—1 yd.
Pink print	—1¾ yd.
Muslin	—8½ yd.
Purple floral print for bias binding	—1¼ yd.
Backing	—7¾ yd.

Number to Cut

Template A	—80 purple floral print
Template B	—80 purple floral print
Template C	—160 green
Template D	—320 pink print
Template E	—640 muslin
Template F	—20 green
Template G	—80 muslin
Template H	—80 pink print
Template I	—12 purple floral print
Template I★	—12 purple floral print
Template J	—12 purple floral print
Template K	—12 purple floral print
Template K★	—12 purple floral print
Template L	—8 purple floral print
Template L★	—8 purple floral print
Template M	—10 purple floral print

★ — Flip or turn over template if fabric is one-sided.

Quilt Top Assembly

1. Join 2 points (E) to the sides of point (D), as shown in Sunburst Piecing Diagram I. Make 16 pieced arcs.

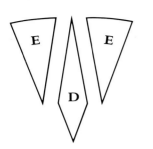

Sunburst Piecing Diagram I

2. Join 2 pieced arcs to sides of point (C), as shown in Sunburst Piecing Diagram II. Join all arcs to make 8 large arcs.

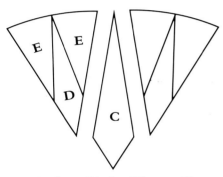

Sunburst Piecing Diagram II

3. Join 2 large arcs to sides of point (B), as shown in Sunburst Piecing Diagram III. Join all arcs to make 4 larger arcs.

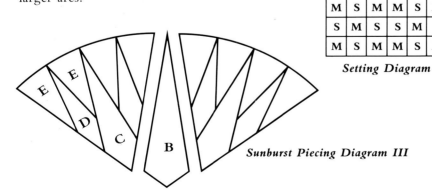

Sunburst Piecing Diagram III

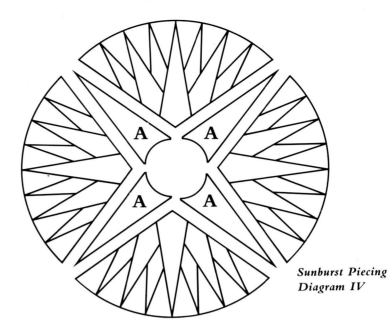

Sunburst Piecing Diagram IV

4. Join larger arcs to sides of 4 points (A), as shown in Sunburst Piecing Diagram IV, to complete sunburst points.

Appliqué 4 petals (H) to circle (F). To aid in appliquéing petals, machine-stitch on seam line before turning edges under. Join circle (F) to center of sunburst.

Complete Sunburst block by joining corner pieces (G) to pieced circle. Make 20 Sunburst blocks.

5. Cut twenty-two 14″ squares from muslin. Alternate muslin

M	S	M	M	S	M
S	M	S	S	M	S
M	S	M	M	S	M
S	M	S	S	M	S
M	S	M	M	S	M
S	M	S	S	M	S
M	S	M	M	S	M

Setting Diagram

squares (M) with Sunburst blocks (S), as shown in Setting Diagram and join at sides to form 7 rows. Join rows.

6. Cut 2 border strips, 5½″ wide, from muslin and join to top and bottom of quilt.

7. Cut 2 border strips, 5½″ wide, from muslin and join to sides of quilt.

8. To aid in appliquéing curves of bow pieces (I, J, K, and L) and swags (M), machine-stitch along seam lines. Pin bows and swags in place before appliquéing, to ensure proper placement. The *top* of each side bow (I) is placed at the midline of each muslin square. Corner bows (I) have four ends (K, L), and the bows are centered on each muslin square. (See quilt drawing.) Appliqué bows and swags. Appliqué knot (J) to bow.

Quilting

Outline-quilt ¼″ inside seam line of each sunburst piece (A-E). Outline-quilt ¼″ outside seam line of appliqué bows and ribbons. Quilt a feathered wreath in each plain muslin square. Quilt the remainder of the quilt in diagonal parallel lines, 1½″ apart.

Finished Edges

Bind with a continuous bias strip of purple floral print fabric.

132

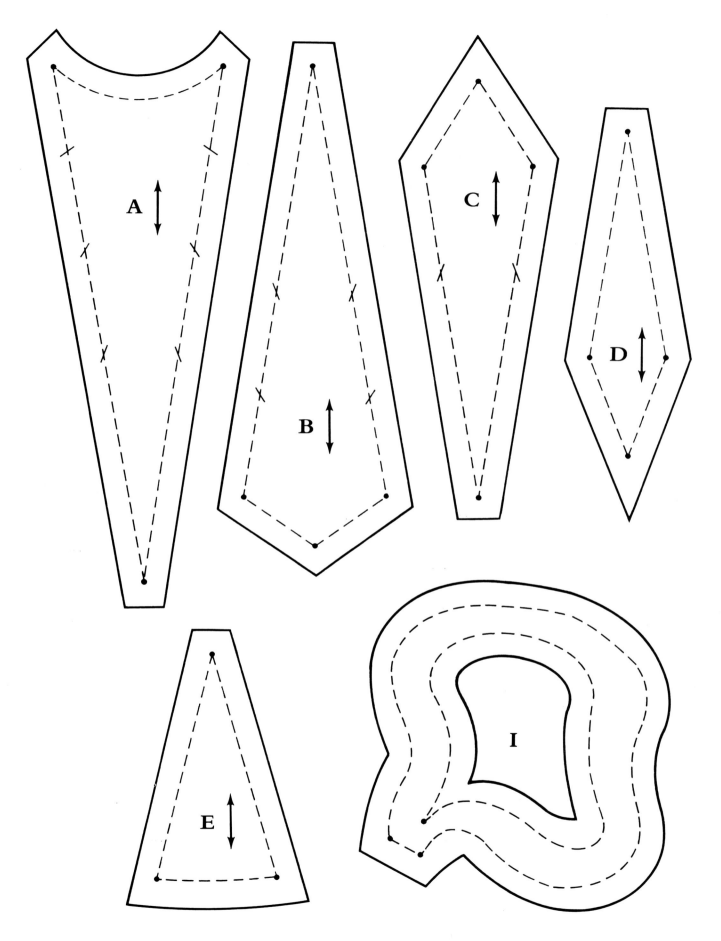

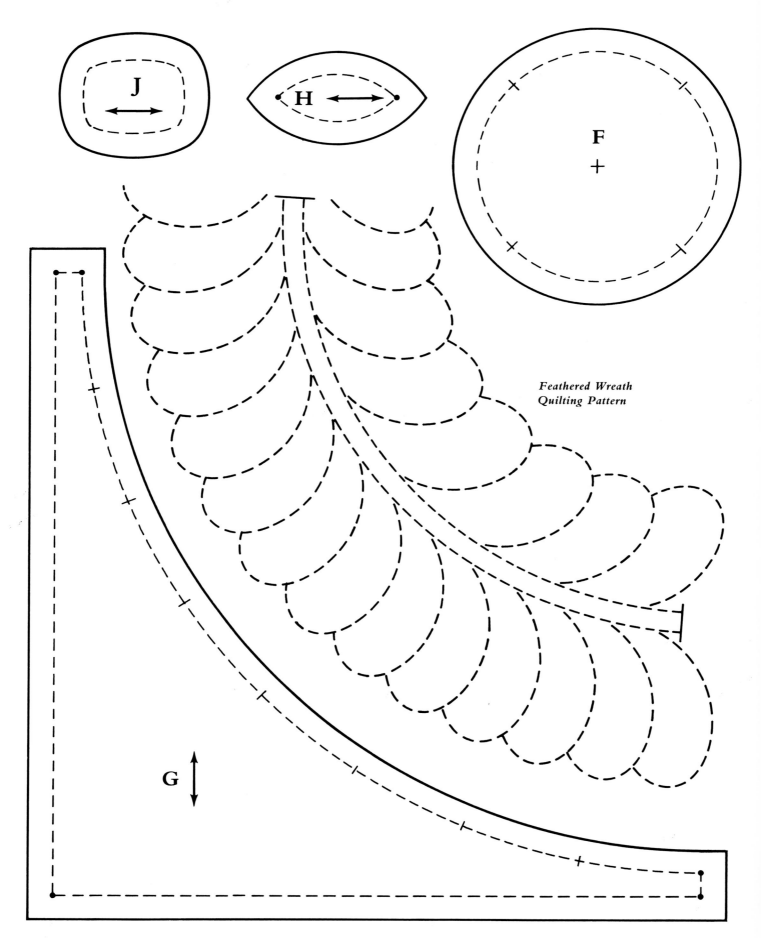

J

H

F

*Feathered Wreath
Quilting Pattern*

G

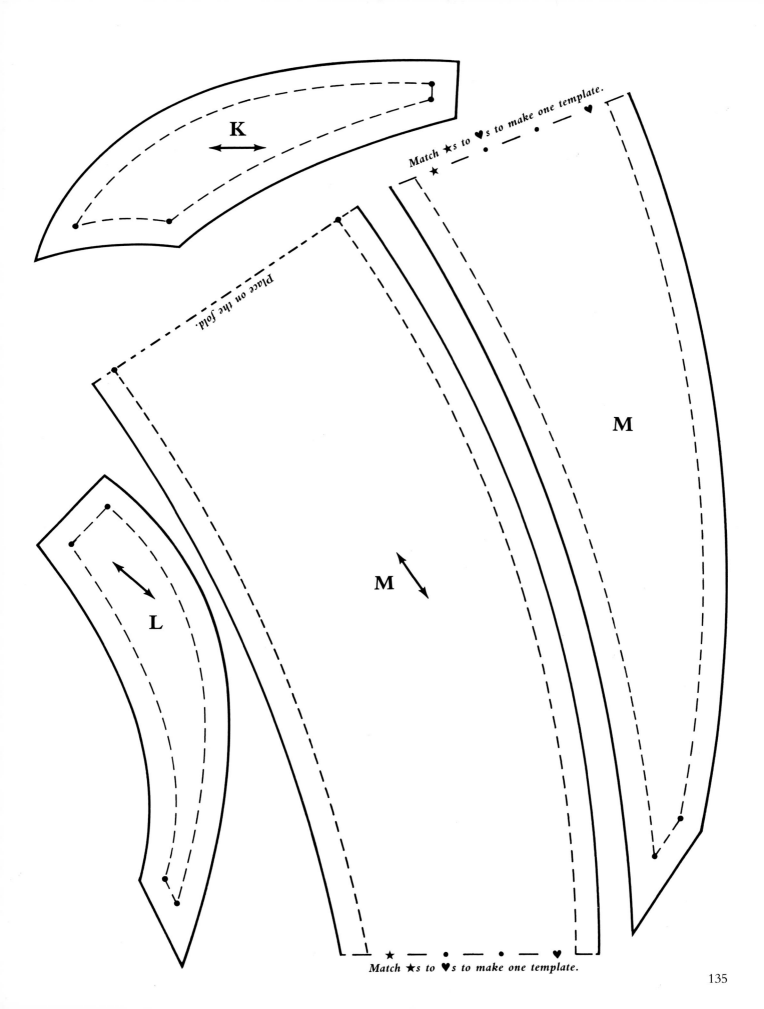

K

Match ★s to ♥s to make one template.

Place on the fold.

M

L

M

Match ★s to ♥s to make one template.

135

DESIGNER GALLERY

It's just to keep me warm, they used to say.
  It's not for show in a gaudy display.
But quilters were masters of their art;
  its radiant beauty grasped at every heart.

Once the fabric industry advanced,
  quilters at last were given a chance.
Ironclad rules of need were destroyed;
  quilting just for necessity was null and void.

Twisting and turning pieces, fabric hues of every shade,
  a fabric executionist is the toast of today's quilting trade.
Exclamations of delight, hoorahs, and pleasing glances,
  for quilts designed and suited for the best of ivory palaces.
Such magnificence, taking center stage—
  quilting as an art form has finally come of age.

Susie Hill & Rachel Leemon

Westover, Alabama

There's always a quilt up at Susie's house. Friends and neighbors recognize it as part of the furnishings. And on quilting days, seated alongside Susie, you can usually find her older sister Rachel quilting away on the latest framed jewel. "Sometimes I pack my bags and stay a night or two," says Rachel, "and we just quilt."

Both have been quilting since they were children. As Susie puts it, "I've been quilting since I was six or eight years old, when my mother bought me a scrap bundle for a nickel."

They both love to tell the story of the time a snow-and-ice storm hit Alabama several years ago. "Rachel was visiting me that day," recalls Susie, "and couldn't go home because the roads were closed. Without much else to do, we started quilting and completed two quilts by lamplight in five days."

Though each keeps a quilt or two of her own going, the fellowship they enjoy while quilting together is irreplaceable.

Robin (standing) *enjoys visiting with Susie* (left) *and Rachel* (right), *especially when there's a quilt in the frame.*

Robin's Ribbon Quilt
1980

Stored in an old shoebox or stashed in the back of a drawer—that's where most of our prize ribbons end up. With good intentions, we say that one day, when we have time, we are going to trot to the framing shop and have them framed. Sound familiar?

Well, *Robin's Ribbon Quilt* solves the problem. Robin is Robin Miller, a young woman and quilter, who has been dairy farming since she was a little girl. Dairy cows are her life, and she has the ribbons to prove it. It was Robin's idea for her lifelong friends Susie and Rachel to make the quilt. And Susie says, teasingly, "She pestered us until we got it made in less than a month!"

Susie and Rachel arranged, pinned, and appliquéd Robin's ribbons on a white sheet. Robin made the initial sketches for the cows, and then Susie, using acrylic paint, completed them and the lettering. (Big M stands for the name of Robin's dairy, and the cow represents the first cow of the dairy.)

It was well worth the effort. In 1980, *Robin's Ribbon Quilt* won first prizes at both the Shelby County Fair in Alabama and the Alabama State Fair. Naturally, Robin cherishes the quilt; it symbolizes years of work and achievement. "Would you believe," says Susie, "that she has enough ribbons to make another quilt?"

Janice Ohlson Richards

Fox Island, Washington

Whether knitting, weaving, or sewing, Janice has been involved in some kind of handwork since childhood. "I have never been able to keep my hands idle," says Janice. Through a series of sketches and trial-and-error piecing on a large flannel cloth, Janice designs her quilts. "I do enjoy that part," she admits, "but the biggest relief is when I can settle in a chair and begin quilting."

Another aspect of quilting that she especially treasures is the number of new friends that she has made because of it. "Quilters are interesting, full of ideas, and super people to know," says Janice enthusiastically.

Having grown up amidst the beauty of the Northwest landscape, Janice says that she is full of inspiration. Even though she quilts for almost 10 hours a week, Janice is looking forward to increasing that time so that more of those great ideas can become finished projects.

Tribute to Tippi Hedren
1984

From sunrise to sunset, swarms of frenzied blackbirds stunned a small seaside village in Alfred Hitchcock's movie *The Birds*. Similarly, Janice's birds appeared to her as unexpectedly as they did to Tippi Hedren and her neighbors in the movie. While Janice was experimenting with the placement of a ten-inch module and with different fabric textures, the image of a bird appeared. Once it did, Janice flipped and angled the module to duplicate the action of flying birds. "It excited me to see the rhythm and pattern of flight emerge," she says.

Luscious corduroys and plain and printed cottons lend the depth and richness required for this landscape of changing light. And whirlpools of quilting accentuate the motion of swirling birds.

Linda Karel Sage

Morgantown, Indiana

Every quilter can relate to the feelings expressed by Linda when she says, "There are always moments of great pleasure in each step of quiltmaking—when a great idea for a quilt comes to you, and when you finally get the fabrics and colors to do what you want them to." She continues, "There's the peacefulness of quilting at the frame, when your mind is free to wander. And the wonderful moment when you hang the quilt up, step back, and really see it."

An accomplished printmaker for many years before she learned to quilt, Linda now challenges herself by trying to make quilts that have a good graphic impact. A viewing wall equipped with flood lamps allows her to view her designs from a distance before assembly. Be sure to enjoy the visual impact of Linda's *Brown County Log Cabins* in the "Quilts Across America" chapter.

Indiana Night Music
1985

In rural Indiana, night music is defined as the insect and frog sounds of the woods. Linda's *Indiana Night Music* visualizes these sounds as bright shapes that pierce the black veil of night and float effortlessly in melodic undulations.

The original block was based on the Amish Rainbow, and strip-piecing methods were used to make the triangles. Linda appliquéd and stuffed each small yellow triangle that tumbles across the quilt. For those of us who don't live close enough to hear the night music, Linda has whetted our senses with a rhapsody of quilted splendor.

Anita Holman Knox

Fort Worth, Texas

Anita is a professional artist and instructor who has combined her painting accomplishments with quilting. "Originally quilting was just a hobby," says Anita, "but it has developed into much more than just a venture to pass the time." In quiltmaking Anita discovered that she was challenged by the same design concepts she found in painting, such as textures, colors, and composition.

Besides simply duplicating her paintings in quilted format, linking the two art forms has opened other avenues. Experimenting with fabric colors as she does paint colors and painting on fabrics are some of the challenges that are similar.

"Quilting has become an integral part of my paintings," says Anita, "and a very important and vital part of my life." She continues, "Like my paintings, quilting is a record of my family, my life, and my interests."

Madonna
1983
Embellishments of lace and satin cording adorn this exquisite contemporary rendition of the Madonna and Child. *Madonna* is a fabric reproduction of Anita's painting, *Madonna* (see below). "I wanted to see if my ideas could be translated into fabric," says Anita. Extensive trapunto strengthens the impact of the fabric Madonna and imitates the subtle gradations of graceful brush strokes.

Ami Simms

Flint, Michigan

Ami Simms is in the midst of an ongoing love affair with quilting. "I love all of it," says Ami. "Should I live to be 104, I will probably never complete all the quilts I'd like to make," she goes on. These days, most of her creative energy is directed toward making pictorial quilts to satisfy her design urge. Her work has been featured in several national magazines and other publications, and has been exhibited in juried competitions in California, Florida, Illinois, Kentucky, Michigan, Tennesseee, Vermont, and Wisconsin. Read more about Ami and her *Whig Rose* quilt in the "Quilts Across America" chapter.

La Strada
©1985

It comes alive! While looking at *La Strada,* one can almost hear the rumbling of cars and the blaring of horns, the rustling of laundry drying in the wind, the sounds of television sets, neighbors visiting neighbors, and a few meows and barks, trailing the screams of playing children. *La Strada* represents Ami's memories of a typical Italian street. "This is a very personal quilt for me," says Ami, "filled with pleasant recollections of living in Italy and of the lovely Italian people who made me feel at home."

Neuschwanstein
©1986

"It's one of those quilts that just had to be made," says Ami. "I've always loved castles; I'm always searching for the perfect one. When I thought of making a castle quilt, photographs of King Ludwig's castle kept popping up everywhere—in travel posters, commercials, and even on the cover of my husband's social studies textbook!"

Varieties of hand-dyed, bleached, and tea-stained fabrics were used to create Ami's version of King Ludwig's castle in Bavaria. In five months, Ami pieced 733 separate shapes and added details with an assortment of embroidered embellishments. *Neuschwanstein* won first place in the Original Design for Wall Hangings—Professional Category at the 17th Annual National Quilting Association Show in 1986.

RESOURCES

Many of our quilters gained inspiration for their quilt designs from previously published designs and patterns. Below is a list of those publications.

Linda Karel Sage's *Brown County Log Cabins*—The cabin pattern is from Mountain Mist Simply Classic Patterns, The Stearns Technical Textiles Company, 100 Williams Street, Cincinnati, OH.

The technique for invisible appliqué was published with permission from Ami Simms. Simms A: *Invisible Appliqué*. Flint, MI. ©1986 by Ami Simms.

Rita Erickson's *Mountain Lake Isa*—Schlotzhauer JM: *The Curved Two-Patch System*. McLean, VA: EPM Publications, Inc., 1982.

Sylvia Whitesides's *Ryan's Quilt*—The cross-stitching patterns were designed by The Vanessa-Ann Collection, P.O. Box 9113, Ogden, UT.

Resources for Books, Supplies, and Fabrics

Many techniques used by quilters, such as screen printing, require lengthy and detailed instructions. Below is a list of recommended books on subjects of interest to quilters. The list is also designed to help quilters locate materials and specialty fabrics not locally available. To avoid confusion regarding prices, availability of materials, or shipping charges, first contact the supplier and request a catalog and complete ordering information.

Information on Screen Printing

Lassiter F, Lassiter N: *Screen Printing: Contemporary Methods and Materials*. Philadelphia, PA: Hunt Manufacturing Co., 1978.

For a free pamphlet, *Screen Printing Instructions,* send a 9″ x 12″ self-addressed envelope to Hunt Manufacturing Company, 1405 Locust Street, Philadelphia, PA 19102. Or check with your local art supply store; they may have copies on hand.

Screen-Printing Supplies

Screen-printing supplies may be obtained from your local art supply store or ordered from a major distributor, such as the one listed below:

Cerulean Blue, Ltd.
P.O. Box 21168
Seattle, WA 98111-3168

Books on Hand-Dyeing Fabric

Myers J: *Color Formulas for Use with Procion® M-Series Reactive Dyes*. Minneapolis, MN. ©1986 by Jan Myers. (Includes instructions for hand-dyeing fabrics.)

Order from:
Jan Myers
4234 Longfellow Avenue
Minneapolis, MN 55407

Millard D: *A Quilter's Guide to Fabric Dyeing*. Englewood, CO. ©1984 by Debra Millard.

Order from:
Debra Millard
7500 South Ulster
Englewood, CO 80112

Supplies for Hand-Dyeing Fabric

Fiber-reactive dyes can be ordered from the following companies:

Textile Resources
10605 Bloomfield Avenue
Los Alamitos, CA 90720

Pro Chemical and Dye Inc.
P.O. Box 14
Somerset, MA 02726

Japanese Fabrics

Mr. Jeffery Cline, President of Kagedo Inc., is happy to work with quilters to obtain the kinds and amounts of Japanese fabrics you need.

Kagedo Inc.
55 Spring Street
Seattle, WA 98104